The Mystical Design
of *Paradise Lost*

The Mystical Design
of *Paradise Lost*

Galbraith Miller Crump

Lewisburg
Bucknell University Press
London: Associated University Presses

Associated University Presses, Inc.
Cranbury, New Jersey 08512

Associated University Presses
108 New Bond Street
London W1Y OQX, England

The author wishes to express his appreciation to The Bobbs-Merrill Company, Inc. for permission to reprint passages from John Milton, *Complete Poems and Major Prose,* edited by Merritt Y. Hughes (New York: The Odyssey Press, 1957).

Library of Congress Cataloging in Publication Data

Crump, Galbraith Miller.
    The mystical design of Paradise lost.

    Bibliography: p.
    1.   Milton, John, 1608–1674.   Paradise lost.
I.   Title
PR3562.C7   821'.4   74–202
ISBN 0–8387–1519–2

PRINTED IN THE UNITED STATES OF AMERICA

For Joan
VIII.489

It may be that universal history is the
history of a handful of metaphors.

Jorge Luis Borges, "The Fearful Sphere of
Pascal," *Labyrinths,* translated by Anthony Kerrigan

CONTENTS

PREFACE

It was almost ten years ago that the idea for this book first occurred to me. I was attempting to assist my students in their reading of *Paradise Lost* by schematizing the major narrative and thematic lines of the poem's development. To my surprise—and no doubt to that of my students as well—I found as my structural sketches multiplied more and more evidence of an elaborately articulated, circular pattern underlying the entire epic. At first I was skeptical of the pattern emerging in my chalk drawings, aware of how easily one can impose, even if subconsciously, one's own formalist tendencies on another's artistry. But after testing my findings against further investigation and research and after exposing them to the critical eye of my students and colleagues over a period of years, I became reasonably satisfied that what I had worked out in relation to *Paradise Lost* suited with the poem, its tradition, and the habits of mind of its creator.

One of the most convincing pieces of evidence that what I was working on was not totally bizarre and idiosyncratic came when I discovered a few years after I had begun my schematization that several other scholars, working independently of each other, had hit upon the same or similar structural principle. Knowledge that others had uncovered what appeared to be the Miltonic design was encouraging and yet, since two of them were already in print, also unsettling. Rather than put aside what I had done, however, I returned to the poem and looked for further implications in the pattern. It was then that I first noted the connections between syntax and structure and the interrelationships between spatial and temporal organization that now form the bulk of the opening and closing chapters of this book. I retain most of my original findings on the physical shape of *Paradise Lost* in chapter 2, even though a not inconsiderable amount of the material presented there has been discussed by Professors John T. Shawcross and J. R. Watson. Despite that, it seems fitting that the complexity of Milton's scheme for his epic appear fully in one place.

Since the events described above, the "story" of my study of the design of *Paradise Lost* becomes predominantly an account of my indebtedness to others who have given generously of their knowledge and time to help me complete this work. In particular, I am deeply grateful to Robert W. Daniel, Louis L. Martz, and Donald L. Rogan, who read various early drafts of this book and made valuable suggestions toward its improvement. Over the years I have received considerable help and encouragement from my students and colleagues, first at Yale University, and more recently at Kenyon College. It would be difficult to acknowledge all who have helped me make this a better book, but among them I wish especially to thank Sheila Blanchard, Harry M. Clor, Patrick Cruttwell, Richard F. Hettlinger, Arthur F. Kinney, Jr., George DeF. Lord, William E. McCulloh, Michael Mott, Ronald A. Sharp, John T. Shawcross, Thomas L. Short, Roger B. Salomon, and Frederick Turner.

The members of the staff of the Bodleian Library, Oxford, the Chalmers Memorial Library, Kenyon, and the Sterling Memorial Library, Yale, have been obliging, generous, and patient in their assistance to me, while the editorial staff and readers at Bucknell have done much to give final shape to this study of shape.

Preface

Last, along with pleasant memories of Provence, my thanks go to Allan W. Grundstrom for introducing me to my publishers, and especially to my wife, Joan, and sons, Andrew, Ian, Patrick, Timothy, and Nicholas for adding the dimensions of life and liveliness to the solemn routine of scholarship.

Galbraith M. Crump

Gambier, Ohio

INTRODUCTION

This essay attempts to define an aspect of *Paradise Lost* that, I believe, has not hitherto been fully studied. It defines a mystical level in Milton's epic related to the more completely investigated and understood levels of the poem's moral, religious, and aesthetic being. By *mystical* I mean to refer specifically to the long tradition of allegorical exegesis that saw sacred literature as created to express a number of levels of meaning, the most mysterious of which was the mystical or anagogical level, which adumbrated God's eternal glory. I shall return to this question in chapter 1. Here let it suffice to say that in *Paradise Lost* the mystical level of meaning is consonant with other readings of the poem and with Milton's poetry, generally speaking. The body of Milton's poetry stresses notions of the poet as prophet, pursuing a career like Virgil's and endowed with a sense of purpose that comes to him through imaginative investigation of the world around him and by intimations of other worlds he cannot actually know. The Virgilian tradition accords well with Milton's ubiquitous sense of a poetic career, shaped in the likeness of that of the great classical master but dedicated to the service of Him whose "State Is Kingly."

From his earliest poetry forward, Milton seems conscious of the interrelationship between sense and shape. One basic problem appears to have been, in this regard, to make the shape organic and not static, to make it unobtrusively lend life and vigor to the statement rather than damp the poetic spark. Though many would disagree, I would suggest, for example, that *L'Allegro* and *Il Penseroso* fail to present a viable form, whereas *Lycidas* succeeds admirably. *L'Allegro* and *Il Penseroso* substitute ingenuity for true poetic mastery. They are preeminently academic poems—even if we read them as parodies of the mind of academe—and much of their charm arises from the intellectual games we can play with them in searching out the parallels, an amusing but ultimately not very rewarding endeavor. In *Lycidas*, on the other hand, Milton has found a form that works by its very unobtrusiveness. Like the hand of God, the action of poetry gives shape to random events, though we cannot always perceive that shape from our mundane point of view. In *Lycidas* the tradition of the pastoral eclogue is the apparent form, the time-tested way of providing consolation. But we mistake if we place too much emphasis on this form. As Joseph Wittreich has suggested, there may be an underlying pattern in *Lycidas* that is more fully responsible for the poem's ultimate aesthetic and mystical power.[1] Although Wittreich himself does not specifically make the point, his discussion of the way the poem's circular rhyme scheme relates to musical patterns suggests a more appropriate tone for the poem than that arising from the pastoral elegy. We might say that Milton recognized the need to imbue his poem with a design that would be more nearly consonant with a Christian vision of harmony, justice, and rebirth. Wittreich suggests that the underlying form of the rhyme scheme of *Lycidas* is the madrigal. If he is right in this, one is tempted to add that Milton's interest in music

1. "Milton's 'Destin'd Urn': The Art of *Lycidas*," *PMLA* 84 (1969): 60–70. For a recent numerological account of the rhyme-scheme and stanza structure of *Lycidas*, which considers the "regenerative power" of the number ten, consult John T. Shawcross's "Some Literary Uses of Numerology," *Hartford Studies in Literature* 1, no. 1 (1969): 50–62.

has served in this case to provide for a poem that *should* be essentially song. No longer is consolation the primary necessity in face of death. An *O Altitudo!* is the more appropriate response to death and loss. It is interesting to me to see as circular the rhyme scheme that shimmers beneath the surface of Milton's poem, like the rays of the rising sun that seem to come from beneath the waters. The pattern suggests the unending life that Edward King has gained through death. His death and the poem thus become images of the perfect plan that exists amid the apparent randomness of life. *L'Allegro* and *Il Penseroso,* taken together, are also circular in form, but the obviousness of the diurnal circularity ultimately stands in the way of thorough aesthetic pleasure.

My point here is not, however, to hold up one poem at the expense of others, and all that I have discussed above is tentative in the extreme. What I really wish to emphasize is that Milton seems successfully to have given shape to *Lycidas,* the later poem, and failed to do so in the earlier ones. Clearly, Milton thought in terms of poetic structures at least as much as he did in terms of genre. But both structure and genre ultimately existed for him as the formalized cartoon exists for the artisan of stained glass, the simple outlines of which he overlays with the emblazonry of beauty and life. However we evaluate Milton's structures, then, we should note both that he seems habitually to be concerned with such formal, aesthetic problems and that in the end *we* admire the brilliance of poetic illumination.

As conscious interest in formal design seems characteristic of Milton's aesthetic point of view, so *Paradise Lost* stands as the preeminent example, I believe, of the shaped poem, of the absolute though unobtrusive consonance between form and meaning. It is "mysteriously meant"—though not in quite the way, I think, Don Cameron Allen has used that Miltonic phrase in describing the history of allegorical ex-

Conclusion is back →

egesis of classical literature.[2] Milton's poem is "mysteriously meant" as Dante intended the *Commedia* to be understood. There is a shape to *Paradise Lost*—both physical and temporal—relating to the narrative or moral levels of the poem, to be sure, but ultimately bespeaking the mystical sense of God's providence and wisdom in working out the affairs of man. The circular design suits well with Renaissance notions of symbol and with modern appraisals of what Northrop Frye calls the "cyclical form of the Classical epic" based on the natural cycles of life and death of persons, civilizations, and worlds. To cite Frye further on the subject, as the Bible is one of those great encyclopedic forms, "probably the most systematically constructed sacred book in the world," which *in toto* "presents a gigantic cycle from creation to apocalypse, within which is the heroic quest of the Messiah from incarnation to apotheosis,"[3] so, to my mind, *Paradise Lost* is another encyclopedic sacred book that develops round the circular image of the eternal, unending providence of God's universe.

In *Paradise Lost* Milton created a vast hieroglyph of God's abundance and love and of man's response to them. Adopting the traditional symbol of God as a point or circle, the center and circumference of all things, Milton fashioned his poem to embody that symbol in its smallest syntactical detail as in its largest structural design. Thus he sought to make his poem consonant with what he believed to be the

---

2. *Mysteriously Meant; The Rediscovery of Pagan Symbolism and Allegorical Interpretation in the Renaissance* (Baltimore, 1970). Professor Allen's book provides an interesting study of exegetical traditions. His vast erudition amply documents the pervasiveness of exegetical concerns in the Renaissance and their continued vitality in Milton's age.

3. *Anatomy of Criticism* (Princeton, 1957), pp. 315–17. Speaking specifically of *Paradise Lost* in *Five Essays on Milton's Epics* (London, 1966), Frye says: "The final point in the vast cycle [of the poem] is the same point as the beginning, yet not the same point, because, as in the *Aeneid*, the ending is the starting point renewed and transformed by the heroic quest of Christ. Thus there can be only one cycle, not an endless series of them" (p. 19). For some recent studies involving the question of the apocalyptic in Milton's art and thought, one might turn to Michael Fixler, *Milton and the Kingdoms of God* (London, 1964), and his "The Apocalypse within *Paradise Lost*," *New Essays on* Paradise Lost, ed. Thomas Kranidas (Berkeley, 1969), pp. 131–78; also see Leland Ryken's *The Apocalyptic Vision in* Paradise Lost (Ithaca, N.Y., 1970).

creative principle of the universe. In *De Doctrina Christiana* (I.ii) Milton had argued that the existence of God could be known in the "many traces of him . . . apparent throughout nature," adding that

> there can be no doubt but that every thing in the world, by the beauty of its order, and the evidence of a determinate and beneficial purpose which pervades it, testifies that some supreme efficient Power must have pre-existed, by which the whole was ordained for a specific end.

Just so, I believe, Milton endowed the world of his poem with as many traces as possible of the circular rhythms of life, both to imitate and intimate the divine presence in all things. On a spiritual level, that is, he sought to imbue *Paradise Lost* with a profound sense of the ultimate wisdom and justice of God's ways.

How Milton set about implementing this aspect of his poem is my subject. Why he chose to do it may be ascertained if we look briefly at the well-known patristic tradition of biblical exegesis that gave rise to it. That tradition recognized four possible levels of meaning in scripture, a literal or historical, an allegorical, a moral, and an anagogical or mystical sense. On the anagogical level the words of the narrative signify that which relates to God's eternal glory. The tradition, which has been exhaustively treated recently by Father Henri de Lubac,[4] probably begins with Philo's commentaries on the Pentateuch. Origen and Augustine develop the method of exegesis in their writings, but it is Aquinas who confirms the fourfold system of interpretation. Beyond the literal level of meaning in which "words signify things," he distinguishes levels of spiritual signification. Speaking of the relationship between the Old and New Testament, he says:

> so far as the things of the Old Law signify the things of the New Law, there is the allegorical sense; so far as the things done in

4. *Exégèse médiévale, les quatre sens de l'Écriture,* 4 vols. (Paris, 1959–64).

Christ, are types of what we ought to do, there is the moral sense. But so far as they signify what relates to eternal glory, there is the anagogical sense.[5]

As Aquinas discusses it, the anagogical sense differs from that tradition of secular *allegoresis* which finds beneath the literal a veiled meaning of hidden truths not always entirely consistent with the apparent surface meaning. The latter was the tradition Sidney had in mind in his *Apology for Poetry* when he said he believed with others that

> it pleased the heavenly Deity by Hesiod and Homer, under the veil of fables, to give us all knowledge, logic, rhetoric, philosophy, natural and moral, and . . . that there are many mysteries contained in poetry, which of purpose were written darkly, lest by profane wits it should be abused.

This is also closer to what Spenser intended by speaking of *The Faerie Queene* as "a continued Allegory, or dark conceit."[6] In the patristic tradition, however, the anagogical sense relates the literal events of this world to that transcendent, eternal pattern of God's glory. The distinction that must be made in this is between the allegory of the theologian and that of the poet. The former deals with historical fact that has mystical significance, while the latter deals with a fiction created to veil an allegorical level. Spenser creates a marvelously complex, fictional narrative to embody his allegory. Milton recounts what were for him the historical facts of the Creation and Fall. Robert Hollander makes the distinction forcefully in his recent study of the *Allegory in Dante's Commedia*:

> to be simple, [the anagogical sense] relates the history of this world to God's; or, it shows that things which have happened

5. The *"Summa Theologica"* of St. Thomas Aquinas, I.i.10, trans. the Fathers of the English Dominican Province (London, 1920), 1: 17.
6. Sidney, *The Defence of Poesie*, etc., ed. Albert Feuillerat (Cambridge, 1923), p. 45; Spenser, *The Poetical Works of Edmund Spenser*, ed. J. C. Smith, (Oxford, 1909), 3: 485.

here point to an afterlife, which is eternal. The point of the anagoge is first to affirm that God's universal plan is operant, that this world is an *umbra futurorum*. In our language we might want to call it the theological sense, which assures us . . . that God is indeed in His heaven. . . . Thus, although the four senses of Scriptural exegesis serve different aims, the medieval system had an enormous attraction because in a single method it found a way of representing history, morality, and metaphysics simultaneously.[7]

To illustrate how the anagoge works, it might be useful to recall Dante's example in his letter to Can Grande della Scala of the exodus of Israel from Egypt. Beyond the historical facts, there is the allegorical level of meaning by which the event signifies man's redemption accomplished in Christ. On the moral level it represents the conversion of the soul from a state of sin to one of grace. Finally, on the anagogical level the event signifies the flight of the sanctified soul from the slavery of this world to the liberty of the everlasting glory in God.

In *Paradise Lost* Milton sought "to justify the ways of God to man," literally, by the narrative of the Creation, Fall, and promise of redemption. Allegorically, the story of the Fall then might be read as a type of the begetting, death, and resurrection of Jesus, the second Adam. Morally, the narrative illustrates the concept of the *felix culpa*, the fortunate

---

7. (Princeton, 1969), pp. 27 and 84 ff. Charles S. Singleton, *Commedia: Elements of Structure, Dante Studies* I (Cambridge, Mass., 1965), p. 15, says: "in the poem, as in the mode of scriptural allegory, the literal sense is given as an historical sense standing in its own right, like Milton's say—not devised in order to convey a hidden truth, but given in the focus of single vision. (Nothing of more importance could happen in Dante criticism at present than a general recognition of this fact.)" Charles Donahue in his "Summation" to the discussion of patristic exegesis contained in *Critical Approaches to Medieval Literature* (*Selected Papers from the English Institute, 1958–59*, ed. Dorothy Bethurum, [New York, 1960], pp. 61–82) defines the basic difference between Greek allegory and the early Christian typological approach to exegesis. "Typology finds a hitherto unsuspected layer of meaning in the original record, but the person, event, or utterance of the record retains all its original existence and value. . . . In the Greek method, the original meaning is destroyed once the allegorical meaning has been discovered. The Athene who pulled Achilles by the hair evaporates into a *bella menzogna* if we say the passage really means that Achilles's prudence restrained his wrath" (pp. 65–66).

Fall, and taught men the need for faith to persevere in the knowledge that God continually brings good out of evil. It follows from this, I would argue, that anagogically *Paradise Lost* expresses the numinous world of eternal life where "no more Change shall be." Unlike the didactic statement of the "Two Cantos of Mutabilitie," however, *Paradise Lost* implies how the cycles of change in the natural world shadow forth our sense of eternal return, a sense that operates in us, as in the epic, below the threshold of consciousness.

There are two further points to note in relation to this tradition. First, the anagogical meaning could be and often was discontinuous in any narrative. There need not be at every moment an anagogical meaning involved in the narrative action before the reader.[8] Second, the danger of presumption on the part of a poet in writing anagogically can be dismissed by reference to the normal sense of the poet as imitator. Charles Singleton speaks to this point in relation to the *Commedia:*

> A poet has not God's power and may not presume to write as He can. But he can *imitate* God's way of writing. He may construct a literal historical sense, a journey beyond (it too happens to be an Exodus!) to be, in the make-believe of his poem, as God's literal sense is in His book (and with God's help he will have the power to make it real).[9]

These remarks could, virtually without alteration, apply to Milton's writing of *Paradise Lost.* Indeed, it is one of the profound, though unnoticed similarities between Dante and Milton, it seems to me, that both fashioned their supreme works with similar artistic assumptions and in the same allegorical tradition.[10]

8. Cf. Augustine's *De Civitate Dei,* xvi. 11.
9. Pp. 15–16.
10. Irene Samuel (*Dante and Milton: The* Commedia *and* Paradise Lost [Ithaca, N.Y., 1966]) does not investigate this aspect of the poems. Of late, numerological studies have linked the two works directly and indirectly, but no one, to my knowledge, has pursued the full implications of the comparison.

Introduction

In the following chapters I hope to demonstrate the pervasiveness of a mystical, that is, anagogical level of meaning in *Paradise Lost,* embodied structurally and conceptually in the form of the circle, which represents both the cyclical rhythms of man's world and the eternal, immutable perfection of the Creator. I will first take up how the pattern impresses itself on the poem thematically and rhetorically. Following that I will discuss how the overall design of the poem reflects the circular motif, actually turning the epic into a giant figure poem. Finally, I will consider the temporal design of *Paradise Lost,* attempting to show how it, too, relates to the circular pattern by which Milton has fashioned one of the most elaborately wrought, beautifully conceived and organized poems in the literature of Western man.[11]

11. It is interesting as well as requisite to note that a number of critics have discussed similar structural features of *Paradise Lost.* Renewed interest in the structure of Milton's epic may be said to have begun with Arthur Barker's essay "Structural Pattern in *Paradise Lost,*" *Philological Quarterly* 28 (1949): 17–30. Barker concluded that Milton's revision of his poem prior to the second edition in 1674 "clarified" its pattern. Slight though they were, the revisions deemphasized the five-act structure of the poem, which owed "so much to neo-classical theory, formulated by the Italians and of great force among Milton's English predecessors." In reorganizing the original ten books into twelve, Milton had moved away from a theory "which closely associated the tragic and epic forms, . . . perfectly exemplifying what were thought to be the Aristotelian requirements of structure." Since Barker's article, the structural design of *Paradise Lost* has received considerable attention. Among those whose work has been most helpful to me in my present undertaking are M. M. Mahood, *Poetry and Humanism* (Port Washington, N. Y., 1950), chap. vi, pp. 169–206; William G. Madsen, "The Idea of Nature in Milton's Poetry," *Three Studies in the Renaissance,* etc., (New Haven, 1958); Isabel Gamble MacCaffrey, Paradise Lost *as "Myth"* (Cambridge, Mass., 1959), chap. 3, pp. 44–91; Jackson Cope, *The Metaphoric Structure of* Paradise Lost (Baltimore, 1962), chaps. iii-iv, pp. 50–148; Anne Davidson Ferry, *Milton's Epic Voice: The Narrator in* Paradise Lost (Cambridge, Mass., 1963), chap. vi, pp. 147–78; J. R. Watson, "Divine Providence and the Structure of *Paradise Lost,*" *Essays in Criticism* 14 (1964): 148–55; John T. Shawcross, "The Balanced Structure of *Paradise Lost,*" *Studies in Philology* 62 (1965): 696–718; and Sheila Blanchard, "Structural Patterns in *Paradise Lost:* Milton's Symmetry and Balance" (dissertation, University of Rochester, 1966).

1

The Creative Pattern

One of the central concepts of *Paradise Lost* both in position and meaning comes in the chorus sung by the Angelic host on the return of the Son from creating the universe, in which they joyously proclaim that "to create/Is greater than created to destroy" (VII.606–7). Here as elsewhere Milton's poem exemplifies the sense of renewal and return, of the grand creative pattern of the cyclical—the sublunar sign of the immutable and eternal. "One of the most convenient hieroglyphics of God," said John Donne, "is a circle, and a circle is endless. Whom God loves, He loves to the end."[1] The circle signifies God's eternal being, His perfection, and the organic scheme of His cosmos, just as "ideo circularitas motus animae completur in hoc quod ad Deum manuducit."[2] In its circularity *Paradise Lost* represents the teleological promise of eternal good in a world seemingly held in the destructive grip of time. It does so, for example, by its narrative emphasis on the accounts of the

1. *The Sermons of John Donne,* ed. E. M. Simpson and George R. Porter (Berkeley, 1953), vi. 173.
2. St. Thomas Aquinas, *In Librum B. Dionysii de Divinis Nominibus,* caput iv. lectio 7. Also see *Summa Theologica,* Secunda Secundae, Q. 180, Art. 6.

various moments of creation suggestive of the continuing aspect of the creative process,[3] by the dramatic energies of conflicting forces—of "contraries" in something like Blake's sense of the word—and by the organic, "circular" nature of the rhetoric and imagery reflecting an essentially hylozoistic concept of the universe, in which life imbues all matter.

Put another way, and over-simply, *Paradise Lost* manifests God's bounty and mercy, while everywhere displaying the vigor of Milton's own faith in the creative processes. Though the poem variously "justifies the ways of God to man," it succeeds most profoundly, it seems to me, by virtue of its own creative abundance, which affirms the constant, creative potential of the cosmos. Confronting the break-up of the traditional limited, spatially defined universe, confronting

the destruction of the cosmos and the geometrization of space, that is, the substitution for the world as a finite and well-ordered whole, in which the spatial structure embodied a hierarchy of perfection and value, that of an indefinite or even infinite universe no longer united by natural subordination, but unified only by the identity of its ultimate and basic components and laws,[4]

Milton wished to "reassert *eternal* providence" (italics added) and demonstrates man's God-given ability to create

3. In *Les Métamorphoses du cercle* (Paris, 1961), Georges Poulet reminds us that

le ciel, la nature, la création tout entière dans son déploiement spatial et temporel, n'on d'existence que parce que partout et toujours l'action d'un centre créature les fait exister. Cette action créatrice est assurément, au premier chef, spatiale, puisque chaque lieu de l'univers est le point d'aboutissement de son action. Mais elle est aussi temporelle, puisque, chaque moment nouveau est aussi l'effet de cette création continué. (p. viii)

Mircea Eliade describes the ways primitive man seeks to affirm the mythic nature of continual creation, or re-creation, in *The Myth of the Eternal Return*, trans. Willard Trask, Bollingen series 46 (New York, 1954) chap. 2, "The Regeneration of Time."

4. Alexandre Koyré, *From the Closed World to the Infinite Universe* (Baltimore, 1957), p. viii.

out of apparent loss a new dimension of time and space. For this reason, as Anne Ferry has pointed out, "the physical order of the universe is circular," whether Ptolemaic or Copernican, "and man is its moral center."[5] Perhaps because he sensed the loss of much of the old world and its aspirations before the incursions of a new world of knowledge and rational optimism, Milton fashioned as perfect a poem as he could, a poem that bore witness in as many ways and as fully as possible not merely to "the ontological attributes of Divinity" (Koyré, p. 276), but to the continuing presence of the creative imagination in the divine scheme.

On the literal level *Paradise Lost* reenacts, of course, the events of the Creation and Fall, at once dramatizing them and making explicit their relation to God's overall plan of redemption for man through Christ made man:

> So Man, as is most just,
> Shall satisfy for Man, be judg'd and die,
> And dying rise, and rising with him raise
> His Brethren, ransom'd with his own dear life.
> So Heav'nly love shall outdo Hellish hate,
> Giving to death, and dying to redeem,
> So dearly to redeem what Hellish hate
> So easily destroy'd, and still destroys
> In those who, when they may, accept not grace.
>   (III. 294–302)

The apocalyptic image of judgment with which Milton has God close also makes clear the moral as well as allegorical meaning in Christ of the total scheme:

> The World shall burn, and from her ashes spring
> New Heav'n and Earth, wherein the just shall dwell
> And after all thir tribulations long
> See golden days, fruitful of golden deeds,

5. *Milton's Epic Voice*, p. 158.

With Joy and Love triumphing, and fair Truth.
. . . .
God shall be All in All.

(III. 334–41)

Like the Platonic year, time would eventually return upon itself and be summed up in eternity. In a syntactically circular passage (e.g., "Giving to death, and dying to redeem"), Milton stresses the circular notion of the overall narrative theme that God would bring good out of evil.

In this light, one of Milton's greatest themes concerns the justification of the creative act. Quite simply, he saw and proclaimed that "God's ways" are creative and that man is most nearly like Him in emulating His creativity. As W. B. C. Watkins notes:

> Of Milton's great themes Creation is most completely and serenely realized in his work. It is closest to his heart. He [like God] is an artificer of the word and no other theme offers him such rich correspondence with all he most prizes. . . . Milton [never] . . . lets us forget from beginning to end the Divine creative process. It is both substance and structure of his epic.[6]

The creative essence of God is something Satan never really understands (cf. VI. 853–69). As a result of the Fall, man pays dearly for the knowledge and must relearn it perennially. But he can learn, and that makes all the difference.

The need to learn the importance of the creative act accounts, in part, for the narrative emphasis Milton places on the processes and moments of creation related to his poem. In contrast to the inorganic or destructive activities of Satan and his crew "creating" the first cannon and building Pandemonium, of Sin's recollection of her creation from Satan's brain and the incestuous aftermath that produced Death, and finally of the "petrific" building of the

6. *An Anatomy of Milton's Verse* (Baton Rouge, 1955), pp. 42–44. Among the many critics who have written incisively about the emphasis on creativity in *Paradise Lost*, I would cite in particular Dame Helen Gardner, *A Reading of Paradise Lost* (Oxford, 1965), and Louis Martz, *The Paradise Within* (New Haven, 1964).

causeway from Hell to the world, stands the truly organic creativity of God. Adam and Eve recall in elaborate and vital detail the moment of their coming into existence—something Satan refuses to do. Raphael recounts for them the abundance of the creation of the new world. Milton considers briefly the creation of the Son by the Father and symbolizes the infusion of life in the world by the lesser sun's benign, penetrative warmth:

> the great Luminary
> Aloof the vulgar Constellations thick,
> That from his Lordly eye keep distance due,
> Dispenses Light from far; they as they move
> Thir Starry dance in numbers that compute
> Days, months, and years, towards his all-cheering Lamp
> Turn swift thir various motions, or are turn'd
> By his Magnetic beam, that gently warms
> The Universe, and to each inward part
> With gentle penetration, though unseen,
> Shoots invisible virtue even to the deep:
> So wondrously was set his Station bright.
> (III. 576–87)

And, from our postlapsarian point of view perhaps most important of all, Milton discusses the creative process of the poem itself. We hear of nightly visitations from the Muse Urania, of the light implanted within him sustaining him when he was close to despair, and we recognize, I believe, that the invocatory passages, the lyric moments of the poem, celebrate God's gift to man of the ability to be creative even in face of loss, to reaffirm his faith and create anew.

Satan acts negatively. His every endeavor violates the principle of creation. He emulates "the outward pomp and show" of things in order to assert selfhood:

> The mind is its own place, and in itself
> Can make a Heav'n of Hell, a Hell of Heav'n.
> What matter where, if I be still the same.
> (I. 254–56)

In so doing, he fails to recognize that the basic principle of creation involves response to otherness, be it between sun and earth, man and wife, poet and poem, God and man. The implications of this failure in relation to creation in general and to the poem in particular have been fully analyzed by Arnold Stein in his discussion of Milton's *Answerable Style.* The career of the infernal trinity, he says,

> constitutes a negative proof that also has some bearing on Milton's attitude toward the imagination; for they oppose, in a mechanical metaphor [i.e., their allegorical being] cut off from true reality, the whole imaginative vision of true creation and the true poem, with its degrees of metaphor leading up to the great source which allows imaginative freedom, under love and order, to the human and natural.[7]

In a supreme irony, Satan and his horde seek to express "imaginative freedom" in building their great council hall, only to construct Pandemonium which, though conceived by the heavenly architect, Mulciber, is nothing more than a parody of Heaven, lit by "many a row/Of Starry Lamps" that "yielded light/As from a sky" (I. 727–30). Whereas the fallen angels make every effort to suggest the organic nature of Pandemonium:

> As in an Organ from one blast of wind
> To many a row of Pipes the sound-board breathes.
> . . . . [it]
> Rose like an Exhalation,
>
> (I. 708–11)

Milton reveals the true nature of their activity in the images of violation by which he describes the work of their "impious hands," which

7. (Minneapolis, 1953), p. 158.

Rifl'd the bowels of thir mother Earth
For Treasures better hid.[8]

Even when Satan interacts with another, as he does with his daughter, Sin, he merely isolates and enforces selfhood. The product of his incestuous affair with Sin is Death.[9] Death in turn engenders in Sin the multitudinous Hell Hounds, those "yelling Monsters that with ceaseless cry/ Surround" her and return "when they list into the Womb/ That bred them" (II. 795–99), providing, in Watkins's words, "a hideous travesty of plenitude" (p. 71).

Such is the abundance of Satan. In contrast to it Milton portrays God's true abundance. As Raphael describes the Creation of the world, he stresses the animation of the process, the sheer exuberance of life that literally springs up before our eyes:

Immediately the Mountains huge appear
Emergent, and thir broad bare backs upheave
Into the Clouds.
                    (VII. 285–87)

Then Herbs of every leaf, that sudden flow'r'd
Op'ning thir various colors, and made gay
Her bosom smelling sweet: and these scarce blown,
Forth flourish'd thick the clust'ring Vine, forth crept
The smelling Gourd, up stood the corny Reed
Embattl'd in her field: and th' humble Shrub,
And Bush with frizzl'd hair implicit: last
Rose as in Dance the stately Trees, and spread
Thir branches hung with copious Fruit.
                    (VII. 317–25)

The grassy Clods now Calv'd, now half appear'd
The Tawny Lion, pawing to get free
His hinder parts, then springs as broke from Bonds,

8. I. 687–88. See Watkins, pp. 71ff. Also Isabel Gamble MacCaffrey, pp. 156ff.
9. For a lively, if exaggerated post-Freudian estimate of Satan's obscene, "uncrea-tive" activities, see Michael Lieb, *The Dialectics of Creation: Patterns of Birth and Regeneration in* Paradise Lost, (Amherst, Mass., 1970), especially pp. 16–34.

> And Rampant shakes his Brindled mane; the Ounce,
> The Libbard, and the Tiger, as the Mole
> Rising, the crumbl'd Earth above them threw
> In Hillocks; the swift Stag from under ground
> Bore up his branching head: scarce from his mould
> *Behemoth* biggest born of Earth upheav'd
> His vastness: Fleec't the Flocks and bleating rose
> As Plants.
>
> (VII. 463–73)

Throughout his hexameral account Milton employs personification and symbiotic simile to create a vital universe. Whereas Satan, Sin, and Death turn on their progenitor, reproducing by a kind of deadly invagination, God blends life forces to create an expressionistic world that burgeons with love for the Creator. In the above passages the verbal emphasis is on "opening," "spreading," "freeing." These are the aspects of birth that symbolize for Milton the essence of being under God.

Though Raphael tells Adam and Eve of God's Creation, we witness, of course, Milton's own vision of Genesis. Steeped in the commentaries on Creation, Milton's natural fascination with the complexities of the life force led him, as Frank Manley shows, to embrace many of the problematical aspects of creation such as the source of hybrid forms.[10] Milton's synthesizing bent is perhaps nowhere more evident than in Book VII, since, in the way he understands the creative act, synthesis is a crucial factor in the outgoing process. Man needs to create not in relation to himself but outwardly, in relation to others. The creative act is, as I have said, a response to otherness, an encompassing process. The contrasting responses of Adam and Eve to their first moments on earth may serve as examples of this point. Eve immediately falls under the spell of her own image (IV. 449–65), whereas Adam responds to the world around him with wonder and praise:

10. "Milton and the Beasts of the Field," *MLN* (1961): 398–403.

Straight toward Heav'n my wond'ring Eyes I turn'd,
And gaz'd a while the ample Sky, till rais'd
By quick instinctive motion up I sprung,
As thitherward endeavoring, and upright
Stood on my feet; about me round I saw
Hill, Dale, and shady Woods, and sunny Plains,
And liquid Lapse of murmuring Streams; by these,
Creatures that liv'd, and mov'd, and walk'd, or flew,
Birds on the branches warbling; all things smil'd,
With fragrance and with joy my heart o'erflow'd.
(VIII. 257–66)

Adam reacts positively. His praise corresponds to his intuitive knowledge of the essence of things, while Eve's Narcissuslike reaction foreshadows her turning away from Adam to aspire to the sovereignty of superior knowledge.

Milton's desire publicly to instruct in God's glory[11] lies behind his presence in his own poem. Rather than as a subordinate theme of lyric concentration, the magnificent passages in which Milton considers the nature of the creative act in relation to his present undertaking should be read as public and dramatic utterances. As such they may be compared to the elaborate soliloquies Satan delivers to exonerate himself. Satan's speeches explain, excuse, and, at times, pity the self, while Milton's celebrate God, praising the creative gift given by Him, the "talent" which years before, at the onset of his blindness, Milton had feared was "lodg'd" with him "useless". Though the bardic presence speculating on the sufficiency of his creative powers in face of the epic task and seeking the Muse's aid is a commonplace in the poetic tradition Milton follows, the speculation and the seeking assume a deeper significance than usual in Milton's treatment of them. Rosalie Colie writes in this regard:

11. "The Reason of Church-Government Urg'd Against Prelaty," *Works* (New York, 1931), 3:22. For an excellent account of the "educative" processes by which Milton recreates the Fall in the mind of the reader so that he falls again as Adam did, "not deceived," see Stanley Eugene Fish, *Surprised by Sin: the Reader in Paradise Lost* (New York, 1967).

Milton recognized his own function as "maker" and his responsibility in the creation of a poetic and moral world. His renaissance humanism honoured the long Neoplatonic tradition of the poet as creator; his Christianity identified him irrevocably with Adam and thus all mankind.[12]

Milton asks the Heavenly Muse, Urania, to instruct him, to illuminate him. In the process he becomes a figure in his poem. He assumes the role of man the poet, the creator. When he compares himself with

> Blind *Thamyris* and blind *Mæonides*,
> And *Tiresias* and *Phineus* Prophets old,
> (III. 35–36)

he establishes a link with the past endeavors of men of vision and "advent'rous song." When he discusses the subject of his epic and compares it with those of the *Iliad* or the *Aeneid*, he involves himself in a critical analysis of fruitful poetic themes. And when he sees a mythic connection between himself and Orpheus or between his imaginative endeavors and Bellerophon's, whose attempt to storm heaven on Pegasus symbolized "intelligence and courage overcoming obstacles,"[13] he recognizes the genuine risks involved in creative aspiration:

> Descend from Heav'n *Urania*. . . .
> . . . .
> Return me to my Native Element:
> Lest from this flying Steed unrein'd, (as once
> *Bellerophon,* though from a lower Clime)
> Dismounted, on th' *Aleian* Field I fall
> Erroneous there to wander and forlorn.
> (VII. 1–20)

12. "Time and Eternity: Paradox and Structure in *Paradise Lost,*" *Journal of the Warburg and Courtauld Institute* 23 (1960): 134. Miss Colie's important essay has contributed much to my thinking about the time-scheme of *Paradise Lost,* considered in chapter 3.
13. Jean Seznec, *Survival of the Pagan Gods,* (New York, 1953), p. 100.

As his narrative concerns the fall of man resulting from his "premature snatching at knowledge,"[14] so his own endeavors to describe the Fall and its implications might yet prove a rash plucking of wisdom too soon, despite the long and patient preparation "while green years" were upon his head.[15]

Man as poet, as creator, sets himself apart from other men, takes a chance, communicating only to a few; he is perhaps affected adversely, as Milton feared, by his advanced age, or the dark and damp climate in which he labors.[16] In creating his epic Milton, like Satan, is adventuring, questing over vast and illimitable spaces, but with this difference. Whereas Satan is always truly alone, defining all from within himself, the creative man looks outward spiritually and seeks divine light. Nowhere are the identification and contrast made more poignantly, to my mind, than in the invocation in Book III. Cross-identifications between Milton and Satan, both newly "escap't the Stygian pool," illuminate the passage and establish superb lyric ironies that contrast the inner light of the blind poet with Satan's inner darkness. In a hymn to "holy Light," Milton

14. The phrase is cited by Kermode, *The Sense of an Ending: Studies in the Theory of Fiction,* (Oxford, 1957), p. 87. It comes from Urs Baltasar's *A Theology of History* (New York, 1963), p. 30. The larger context of the quotation is here:

> God intended man to have all good, but in His, God's time; and therefore all disobedience, all sin, consists essentially in breaking out of time. Hence the restoration of order by the Son of God had to be the annulment of that premature snatching at knowledge, the beating down of the hand outstretched towards eternity, the repentant return from a false, swift transfer into eternity, to a true, slow confinement in time.

Along with *Paradise Lost, Lycidas* provides an interesting manifestation, among many to be found in Milton's writings, of a deep consciousness of the priorities and proprieties of time in the mortal scheme of things.

15. "The Reason of Church-Government Urg'd Against Prelaty," p. 617.

16. *Paradise Lost,* IX. 41–47. Among the critics who have recently discussed the role of the poet in his poem, I have found Louis Martz, *The Paradise Within,* pp. 105–10, and Helen Gardner, *A Reading of Paradise Lost,* pp. 35–37, particularly helpful. Miss Gardner notes in passing that the force of the poet's presence has made some critics "assert that Milton is the true hero of his own epic, conducting a war *à l'outrance* on Satan, the creation of his own imagination."

flies upward on "bolder wing" from the darkness of "eternal night," and as we comprehend his flight, we realize that we have made a visual substitution of the poet for Satan, whom we had been watching beat his way upward from Hell to the "glimmering dawn." As Milton manages the substitution, he prepares us for a more complex pattern of parallels and contrasts. Darkness benights both Satan and the poet. Both represent "fallen" creatures who keenly sense their loss and react to it. Satan flies upward to destroy others, to act on them for their loss; Milton to create, to provide others with a pattern to emulate for their gain. The more detail we receive about the poet as man—living alone in Restoration London, hearing the cries of the revelers at night in the streets below him (these, too, are nightly visitations), confronting not only his loss of sight but the apparent end of all his hopes for England and the Commonwealth—the more we come to see, of course, less Milton the poet than the dramatically conceived figure of modern man. At times he is like Satan, the pent-up city dweller seeking the fresh fields on a "Summer's Morn," but always he is the successor to Adam, reacting to the need for creative faith. Though to Milton the physical aspects of the cycles of the year, the season, and the day have been denied him by his blindness, he does not despair. Like Adam after the Fall, Milton accepts the "dark night of the soul" and all that it implies about man's need for inward light:

> thou Celestial Light
> Shine inward, and the mind through all her powers
> Irradiate, there plant eyes, all mist from thence
> Purge and disperse, that I may see and tell
> Of things invisible to mortal sight.
> (III. 51–55)

The creative act itself becomes the epic act. As Milton creates successfully, so does he demonstrate man's ability to create out of apparent loss. *Paradise Lost* is both product and image of the creative act, as is Adam's final response to the vision of the future and the demands of faith in the praise of God's creative design:

> O goodness infinite, goodness immense!
> That all this good of evil shall produce,
> And evil turn to good; more wonderful
> Than that which by creation first brought forth
> Light out of darkness!
> (XII. 469–73)

The great world of the universe and the little world of the poem have been drawn similarly to teach and delight; Adam's response to Raphael's discussion of the hierarchical pattern makes clear the relationship between knowledge and creation:

> Well hast thou taught the way that might direct
> Our knowledge, and the scale of Nature set
> *From centre to circumference,* whereon
> In contemplation of created things
> By steps we may ascend to God.
> (V. 508–12; emphasis added)

For both worlds the creative act involves the geometric perfection of a master builder:

> and in his hand
> He took the golden Compasses, prepar'd
> In God's Eternal store, to circumscribe
> This Universe, and all created things:
> One foot he centred, and the other turn'd
> Round through the vast profundity obscure,
> And said, Thus far extend, thus far thy bounds,
> This be thy just Circumference, O World.
> (VII. 224–31)

While the theme of creation provides one of the major manifestations in *Paradise Lost* of the sense of renewal by which we perceive the "shape" and meaning of eternal goodness, Milton emphasizes this truth on the mystical level of his poem with innumerable rhetorical and structural touches that adumbrate the circular dynamics of the universe. The poem turns vortexlike through a system of opposing forces that induce motion toward the center. "Without contraries is no progression," said Blake in *The Marriage of Heaven and Hell,* and proceeded to expound his "diabolical" reading of *Paradise Lost.* "Attraction and Repulsion, Reason and Energy, Love and Hate, are necessary to human existence. From the contraries spring what the religious call Good & Evil."[17] Though Milton would not have stated it this way, he presumably recognized some such dynamic pattern in the universe and sought to make an expression of it central to the dramatic energy of his poem. But the contraries do not simply work against each other along a linear line of force. They involve each other, turn on each other, just as in the fallen world:

> Day and Night,
> Seed-time and Harvest, Heat and hoary Frost
> Shall hold thir course.
>
> (XI. 898–900)

Critics have long recognized how internal balance, the use of parallel and corresponding passages, and the development of significant contrasts make important contributions to the symbolism of *Paradise Lost.*[18] Perhaps drawing something from the Pythagoreans' fondness for seeing things in pairs of opposites—such as rest:motion, light:dark, good:evil—Milton's tendency to balance off opposites relates to the overall symmetry of the poem, about

17. *The Prophetic Writings of William Blake,* ed. D. J. Sloss and J. P. R. Wallis (Oxford, 1926), 1: 13.
18. See, for example, B. Rajan, Paradise Lost *and the Seventeenth-Century Reader* (London, 1947), p. 52: "The sustained massing of comparison and contrast, the moral enrichment of every theme by its analogue" helped to define for the seventeenth-century audience "that struggle of light with darkness which the Providence of God administers in history."

which I shall speak in the next chapter, just as the symmetry itself relates to the balanced cosmos imaginatively conceived by Milton from Aristotelian-Ptolemaic principles to suit his needs. Of these opposing or interacting forces—Satan:God, Evil:Good, Death:Life, Darkness:Light, Earth:Sun—none is more dramatically conceived, I think, than the interaction or interpenetration achieved by Milton of time and space. As I hope to demonstrate later, the imposing shape of the poem affirms the eternal being of God. It defines the "shape" of His time by embracing within it all rectilinear time from Creation to the end of the world, by setting the end of things as man can know them in direct relation to the beginning. In the great spatial and temporal scheme, the opposing forces of Good and Evil surround man, whom God has created in His own image and set at the center of the universe. Man thus becomes for Milton the central point round whom a vast and dynamic field of attraction and repulsion operates, the image of God at the still center of all being.

Signs of this kind of kinetic activity exist even in the smallest elements of the epic's syntactical, rhetorical, and imagistic make-up. They contribute to a pervasive rhythm and circularity that bespeak the mystical level of meaning in the poem. Milton has made the least thing contribute to his creative design in much the way he understood God to have done in His universe. If God had created a universe that "in all things" was witness to His divine order, if He had created a universe in which all matter was infused with the life principle, so Milton's poem, in attempting to mirror God's plan, ought to be poetically hylozoistic.

To this end, I believe, Milton endeavors to make his language largely an expression of the organic nature of the cosmos by means of circular rhythms and syntax. It is usual to defend Milton's style either in terms of his concern for Latinate structure, for what the Italians called *latinità in volgare* and recommended as appropriate to the heroic style, or (and this is similar) in terms of the special needs of the "modern" epic poet who must shape his language in such a way that it will lend his poem something of the solemnity and magnitude of the ceremonial occasion of the spoken or "primary epic."[19] Both arguments suggest ultimately that the epic poet must create a style to achieve a celebrative tone in a poem that will be read privately. In *Paradise Lost,* the argument goes, the formal Latinate structure imparted to the language, the height of the rhetoric, the "invented" words, phrases, and patterns, all contribute to fashion a "magniloquence" suitable to Milton's lofty design. Though I accept these analyses of the function of language in *Paradise Lost,* I would shift the emphasis away from the power of the language to recapture the force of the bardic voice, stressing, rather, the symbolic quality of the poetic rhythms. As critics have demonstrated, the great forward pressure of Milton's verse marks the relentless, linear movement of time. In reading *Paradise Lost* we do not simply witness the passage of time like the lotus eaters, unconcerned and unaffected. We experience its forward thrust. Yet the Latinate structure of the verse sentences simultaneously produces circularity. Commenting on Matthew Arnold's phrase about the "self-retarding movement" of the verse, Christopher Ricks notes that though "one of the movements drives forward, the other is circling on itself"[20] and later observes how the Latinate syntax can

---

19. F. T. Prince, *The Italian Element in Milton's Verse* (Oxford, 1954), discusses the influence of Carlo Bembo on the development of a "modern" heroic style:

> The distinction between words and the arrangement of words, between vocabulary and idiom, thus stands at the head of Bembo's critical analysis, and makes possible the chief literary effort of the century, the cultivation of that *latinità in volgare* to which we find a parallel in Milton. Without the example of Bembo's followers Milton would never have succeeded as he did in forming his epic diction." (p. 10)

Of modern critics who have discussed the needs of the epic poet in a literary as opposed to oral tradition, C. S. Lewis may stand as representative (*A Preface to Paradise Lost,* [Oxford, 1942], chaps. 3–7). It is interesting to note that his arguments are not very different in concept from those of the Italian Renaissance.

20. Christopher Ricks, *Milton's Grand Style* (Oxford, 1963), p. 36.

maintain "suspense" as we are "made to wait" in order to
know the full meaning of a passage (p. 46). We can see how
Milton produces in us, through the syntax of the verse
sentence and the structure of the poem as a whole, both an
awareness of man's temporal confinement and also a feeling of assurance that comes with the cyclical sense of "return."[21] The opening lines of the poem establish these
tensions of movement:

> Of Man's First Disobedience, and the Fruit
> Of that Forbidden Tree, whose mortal taste
> Brought Death into the World, and all our woe,
> With loss of *Eden,* till one greater Man
> Restore us, and regain the blissful Seat,
> Sing Heav'nly Muse.
>
> (I. 1–6)

The emphasis is forward to the celebrative verb "Sing,"
which draws all into it and yet suggests a new forward
cadence; but within the lines that lead up to it we note the
anticlimactic progression in the phrases "Brought Death,"
"all our woe," and "loss of Eden," against which stands the
climactic or rising notation of the next phrases, "till one
greater Man/Restore us, and regain the blissful Seat." The
rising and falling notations describe the circular movement
of man's fortunes through time. More than this, I would
suggest that Milton endeavors here, and elsewhere, to have
the verbal structure emphasize the meaning, much as Hopkins does so beautifully in *Spring and Fall: To a Young Child.*
In that lyric he develops a complex pattern of inversion that
creates a kind of syntactical mimesis of our sense of mortality. Thus Hopkins makes tangible the sense of diminish-
ment and loss that Margaret feels but cannot name as she
confronts the gold of autumn.

But if we look more closely at the opening lines of *Paradise Lost,* we can see another aspect of the circularity I have

21. On the reader's relationship to the poem, see Stanley Fish, *Surprised by Sin.*

been discussing. The entire first verse sentence extends beyond the middle of line twelve:

> Of Man's First Disobedience, and the Fruit
> Of that Forbidden Tree, whose mortal taste
> Brought Death into the World, and all our woe,
> With loss of *Eden*, till one greater Man
> Restore us, and regain the blissful Seat,
> Sing Heav'nly Muse, that on the secret top
> Of *Oreb*, or of *Sinai*, didst inspire
> That Shepherd, who first taught the chosen Seed,
> In the Beginning how the Heav'ns and Earth
> Rose out of *Chaos*.

At the syntactical center of this sentence, Milton places the subject, "Heav'nly Muse." Moving in toward the center and then out from it is a pattern of clauses and phrases that describes historical and metahistorical cycles of loss and gain. Rhetorically, the sentence may be likened to antimetabole, a figure of speech in which words and ideas are repeated in inverse order. At the center is the subject and its pronominal substitute, "Heav'nly Muse, that." On either side of this cluster stand the predicates, "Sing" and "didst inspire." Still working away from the center, we find comparable motifs of restoration and teaching through shepherd Man, be he Jesus or Moses. Finally, the passage begins and ends with references to Death and Chaos, historical and metahistorical beginnings. The whole passage may be likened to the cosmos in which God is the still center. At the furthest reaches from him are the regions of Death and Chaos, of loss and pain, which can and shall be eradicated by sacrifice, faith, and knowledge, bringing man ever closer to the perfection of God, his "Heav'nly Muse" whose ways, like Milton's own, are both song and inspiration.

Similarly, throughout *Paradise Lost* Milton stimulates our awareness of the cyclical promise of restoration by the circularity of the periodic, Latinate verse sentence. Describing Adam and Eve for the first time, Milton presents them to us as

> hand in hand they pass'd, the loveliest pair
> That ever since in love's imbraces met,
> *Adam* the goodliest man of men since born
> His Sons, the fairest of her Daughters *Eve.*
> (IV. 321-24)

The first two lines confront us with an intricate time scheme, typical of the poem's mythic pattern of reference. Milton introduces Adam and Eve strolling by us as if in the present but achieves a proper historical perspective by means of the conventional descriptive past tense. He also simultaneously looks forward in time from Eden to compare future lovers with the primal pair. Yet our point of view remains dominant and allows Milton finally to turn time once again back on itself in the past of "met." The shifts in time suggest its plasticity in the hands of the poet, as in those of God, and point to its cyclical nature as the primary element in its plasticity. Milton stresses the circularity of the entire structure in the following two lines, which begin and end with reference to Adam and Eve, who quite literally comprehend between them, as do the lines, all the future progeny of sons and daughters.

Appropriately, in the closing lines of his epic Milton introduces a number of circular notations, some slightly muted perhaps, but all together lending the passage a strong sense of the restorative promise to be felt in the very midst of the forward movement down and out of Eden. In the final verse sentence Milton pictures Adam and Eve looking back. They "all [2] th'Eastern side [1] beheld [2] Of Paradise" and saw "the Gate/With [2] dreadful Faces [1] throng'd and [2] fiery Arms." The verbal clusters relate a feeling of loss or fear, but the encircling action of the language softens the starkness of the vision. Milton goes on to describe the response of Adam and Eve, again with a circular construction: "[3] Some [2] natural tears [1] they dropp'd, but [1] wip'd [2] them [3] soon." The final four lines reinforce the pattern. The first two are repetitive, linear in emphasis, somewhat urgent, though the assurance that "Providence [is] thir guide" suffices to allay the anxieties of "where to choose/Their place of rest." The completing movement of the final lines, moreover, depicts the somber steps through Eden, but with the human assurance of linked hands and the mysterious feeling that though they move "with [2] wand'ring [1] steps and [2] slow", those steps are mystically as well as verbally modified by a kind of celestial syntax strong in the promise of return.

Reinforcing the circularity of the Latinate syntax, which interacts with the forward thrust of its energy, the imagery also tends to inscribe circles by means of anticipation. Describing this kind of image as proleptic, James Whaler notes that the "function of anticipating event in the fable by means of simile seems to be distinctive with Milton" among epic writers. Finding that Milton's "similes at first sight digressive prove under analysis to be beautifully symmetrical," Whaler adds that

> one need not be surprised at similes which are fully interpretable only through a knowledge of the completed fable. We learn, as Milton intended we should learn, to expect homologues; and when he inserts an anticipatory homologue in a complex simile, as he does a fair number of times, the phenomenon is to be deemed as neither oversight nor incongruity nor inspired accident, but a well-considered part of his narrative technique.[22]

Conceptually, the proleptic image probably owes a great deal to the typological habits of mind Milton was heir

22. "The Miltonic Simile," *PMLA* 46 (1931): 1036, 1042.

to;[23] psychically, it provides an ameliorating, metahistorical sense of the cyclical in face of what Mircea Eliade calls "the terror of history"—the force of linear time.[24] Milton's similes reinforce our mythic sense of renewal by both reflection and anticipation. Milton's poem depicts the archetypal action of rebellion and fall, and thus calls into being by way of comparison its future analogues, setting the one, local story in relation to all the future images of man's endeavors to exist in a world of time and loss called forth by his original failure.

One of the most beautiful passages of this kind, where broad verbal rhythms dominate, comes just before the Fall, when Satan suddenly spies Eve "Veil'd in a Cloud of Fragrance"

> the Roses bushing round
> About her glow'd, oft stooping to support
> Each Flow'r of slender stalk, whose head though gay
> Carnation, Purple, Azure, or speckt with Gold,
> Hung drooping unsustain'd, them she upstays
> Gently with Myrtle band, mindless the while,
> Herself, though fairest unsupported Flow'r,
> From her best prop so far, and storm so nigh.
> Nearer he drew. . . .
> Spot more delicious than those Gardens feign'd
> Or of reviv'd *Adonis*, or renown'd
> *Alcinoüs*, host of old *Laertes'* Son,

23. See William G. Madsen, *From Shadowy Types to Truth: Studies in Milton's Symbolism* (New Haven, 1968). Madsen says "that the doctrine of typology throws more light on the symbolic structure of the major poems as well as on Milton's philosophical and religious presuppositions than do the currently fashionable theories about metaphoric or mythic structure and Neoplatonic *allegoria.* . . . In its narrowest sense the theory of typology states that certain persons, things, and events of the Old Testament are symbolic prefigurations, 'shadows,' or types of certain persons, things, and events of the New Testament. Thus Joshua is a type of Christ, who is the antitype; the synagogue a type of the Christian Church; the sacrifice of Isaac a type of the Crucifixion" (pp. 2–3).
24. Eliade shows how "men in the traditional civilizations tolerated history . . . by periodically abolishing it through repetition of the cosmogony and a periodic regeneration of time or by giving historical events a metahistorical meaning, a meaning that was not only consoling but was above all coherent." pp. 141–42.

Or that, not Mystic, where the Sapient King
Held dalliance with his fair *Egyptian* Spouse.
Much hee the Place admir'd, the Person more
As one who long in populous City pent,
Where Houses thick and Sewers annoy the Air,
Forth issuing on a Summer's Morn to breathe
Among the pleasant Villages and Farms
Adjoin'd, from each thing met conceives delight,
The smell of Grain, or tedded Grass, or Kine,
Or Dairy, each rural sight, each rural sound;
If chance with Nymphlike step fair Virgin pass,
What pleasing seem'd, for her now pleases more,
She most, and in her look sums all Delight.
Such Pleasure took the Serpent to behold
This Flow'ry Plat, the sweet recess of *Eve*
Thus early, thus alone.

                    (IX. 426–57)

Much of insight has been written about these lines, which
are among the richest in the poem. The image haunts us
with its allusions and moves us with its sensuality; it actively
equates memory and desire. The opening lines may be said
to be almost entirely sensuous in their appeal, Rubenslike
in color and richness. Roses encircle Eve, as will the impending "storm" that threatens in Satan. The lines themselves describe her act of sustaining the flowers, "stooping
to support them," leading us back to the recognition that
she is the "fairest unsupported flower." As she reaches out
to gather the flowers in her hand, circling them with a
myrtle band, so Milton describes the action and its implications in a verse sentence that returns and encompasses,
though the circular image is, in a sense, pierced by the
direct, forward thrust of "nearer he drew."

The description of the famous gardens of the future has
been elaborately discussed by Milton scholars. The point to
make here is that the allusions look forward in time to the
mythic and real gardens that from our point of view are in
the past. The tension of past, present, and future that Mil-

ton catches at such moments is typical of the particular quality of the proleptic image, by which we achieve something of the divine overview of time. The future is not simply time to come, however, as the comparison makes manifest. It is potentially present at every moment as it serves to bring about apparent repetitions of the specific act we are witnessing in Eden. There will be beautiful gardens in the future, fabled places of love and beauty and loss. Once thrown into time, however, all our acts seem to repeat past and presage future actions. Man lives out the tiny line of his life and engages in the same endeavors as have his ancestors. Nothing changes, though all is change for each man. In this context, Christopher Ricks observes how the allusion to Solomon and Pharaoh's daughter "includes more than beauty: it recalls how a man of great wisdom showed his famous inability to resist a woman. Solomon is a type of Adam, and the allusion has the oblique but powerful purpose of predicting the Fall" (p. 134). We look forward both, in history, to acts that repeat the archetypal act of uxoriousness and, in the local action, to the Fall, which has been foreshadowed. Yet, by the reference Milton also recalls an earlier allusion to Solomon, "Beguil'd by fair idolatresses" (I. 444–46), and thus establishes an echo from the poem's past that emphasizes less the uniqueness of the act than the way it is repeated throughout time. A similar effect has been achieved in the lines just prior to the passage presently under discussion, which compare floral Eve to "*Ceres* in her prime" and recall the comparisons of Eve to Ceres' daughter and Eden to "that fair field of Enna" employed by Milton in Book IV. In both instances the movement is forward, backward—circular. The progress forward in fact has been shown to be cyclical in essence.

Beyond this, Milton follows the reference to Solomon with a rhetorically patterned clause, "Much hee the Place admir'd, the Person more," in which the pronoun refers easily to Satan as he observes Eve and to Solomon, whose image persists so that we identify him, too, as preferring the Person to the Place. Past and present merge with the future, as well, by anticipating Adam's choice and establishing a link between it and the modern city dweller's morning in the country. The complexity of reference also works to situate the reader imaginatively in something like the central position held by the pronoun "hee," as we look back wistfully and forward anxiously. Milton emphasizes the movement by circular word-order:

(1) Much hee (2) the Place (3) admir'd, (2) the Person (1) more.

The antimetabole here would be of little interest were it not related so clearly to the overall meaning and structure of the passage at hand. It calls attention to itself in a way that seems to preclude mere chance as an explanation of its presence. Sufficient examples of this stylistic device can be adduced from *Paradise Lost*, moreover, to support the notion that Milton employed it consciously. The opening verse paragraphs of the poem employ the device with enough frequency to establish its rhythm firmly in our subconscious, at least. I have already spoken of how the rising and falling pattern in the opening lines describes the circular movement of man's lot through time, from disobedience to restoration. It is worth pointing out, as well, how certain phrases also produce a sense of circularity. Note, for example, the effect of the following: "th' [1] upright [2] heart and [1] pure," and " [1] to fall off [2] From thir Creator, and [1] transgress his Will". I shall return to a fuller discussion of such syntactical peculiarities in a moment, but here it is sufficient to point out how they contribute to a sense of circularity, which is reinforced by being placed in conjunction with more elaborate patterns. In describing Satan's aspiration to set himself above his peers, Milton says,

He trusted to have equall'd the most High,
If he oppos'd; and with ambitious aim
Against the Throne and Monarchy of God
Rais'd impious War in Heav'n and Battle proud
With vain attempt.

(I. 40–44)

The passage embodies three separate examples of circular phrasing, which combine to create one larger pattern. The first develops in the opening two clauses, which embed the enterprise "to have equall'd the most High" within statements of Satan's self-confidence and opposition. Likewise, the comparable phrases "with ambitious aim" and "with vain attempt" contain within them a more elaborately spelled-out description of that "vain attempt" to equal "the most High." Completing the complexity of the structure, moreover, Milton introduces the circular pattern of line 43 as follows:

Rais'd (1) impious (2) War in (3) Heav'n and (2) Battle (1) proud

which provides a visual as well as conceptual image of the place, the event, and the quality of Satan's uprising.

There are numerous other examples of this kind of verbal device. At the end of *Paradise Lost,* for example, Eve expresses her new sense of love for Adam and of her place in the divine scheme of things through circular syntax:

with thee to go,
Is to stay here; without thee here to stay,
Is to go hence unwilling; thou to mee
Art all things under Heav'n, all places thou.

(XII. 615–18)

In locating Eden anew in Adam, Eve voices her appropriate version of the "paradise within . . . happier far" that Adam has come to appreciate. Her speech establishes verbally a pattern that circles three times about the verb that indicates her essential being, her positive temporal existence. Adam has become her Eden. Thus in saying " [1] with thee [2] to go, [3] Is [2] to stay [1] here" she has encompassed her being within the comforting and protective presence of her place in Adam. She repeats the statement—and the syntax —three times. It is just possible, it seems to me, that Milton meant to suggest by means of this threefold repetition Eve's absolute relationship through Adam to God, similar to that expressed by Adam before the Fall (IV. 299).

Milton earlier characterizes the state of the fallen angels by an antimetabolic pattern. The fallen angels endure a living death; Milton describes their lot graphically as well as conceptually, for they inhabit

> A Universe of death, which God by curse
> Created evil, for evil only good,
> Where all *life dies, death lives,* and Nature breeds,
> Perverse, all monstrous, all prodigious things.
> (II. 622–25; emphasis added)

In place of the "pure Empyrean" where God sits, Satan views his realm to be a "dismal Situation waste and wild/A Dungeon horrible" (I. 60–61). His situation is a dungeon; both are literally defined by the encircling elements of horror and dismay. This is Satan's first glimpse of the Hell he will become, his first intimation that his thoughts will stir "The Hell within Him, for within him Hell/He brings" (IV. 20–21). Even in his grandest utterances, he will be caught in and become his own labyrinthian rhetoric:

> Hail horrors, hail
> Infernal world, and thou profoundest Hell
> Receive thy new Possessor: One who brings
> A mind not to be chang'd by Place or Time.
> The mind is its own place, and in itself
> Can make a *Heav'n of Hell, a Hell of Heav'n.*
> (I. 250–55: emphasis added)

Circular or labyrinthian entanglement also defines the general fallen state. Thus Milton considers those of "thoughts more elevate" among Satan's followers who

> reason'd high
> Of Providence, Foreknowledge, Will, and Fate,
> Fixt Fate, Free Will, Foreknowledge absolute.
> (II. 558–60)

Critics have recognized how "to humour perplexity" Milton makes "a kind of labyrinth in the very words that describe" the activities of the fallen angels.[25] Certainly it is hard to avoid the feeling that Milton has carefully developed the word order here to manifest the mazelike situation of the damned; I would point out that God also speaks circles. The lines quoted above may more appropriately describe the circularity of God's way in which Satan's followers remain involved. Characterized originally by Satan as those "That durst [1] dislike [2] his reign, and [2] mee [1] preferring" (I. 102), the fallen now find themselves "in wand'ring mazes lost," at once the mark of their situation and the sign of God's supremacy. Eve again expresses herself in a circular manner after the Fall, when she suggests to Adam as a remedy to their pain,

> Let us (1) seek (2) Death, or (2) he (1) not found, supply
> With our own hands his Office.
> (X. 1001–2)

And Milton, at the midpoint of his poem, voices renewed confidence in his ability to go forward with the aid of the Heavenly Muse Urania,

> (1) though fall'n (2) on evil days,
> (2) On evil days (1) though fall'n, and evil tongues.
> (VII. 25–26)

25. Addison, *The Tatler*, no. 114, (31 December 1709); see Ricks, pp. 78–79.

The pertinence of the verbal pattern to the divine schema finds its best expression, however, in God's own statements. Describing His plan for man's salvation, he notes that

(1) Man (2) shall not quite be lost, but (2) sav'd (1) who will,
(III. 173)

and later elaborates on the relationship between His grace and man's redemption, saying that

Upheld by me, yet once more he shall stand
On even ground against his mortal foe,
By me upheld.
(III. 178–80; emphasis added)

In response to the Father, the Son offers Himself as man's ransom, justifying his actions by an observation that continues the syntactical emphasis of return:

(1) man (2) shall find (3) grace;
And shall (3) grace (2) not find (1) means.
(III. 227–28)

Thus the overall plan to bring good out of evil, creation out of chaos, is itself the reversal of the hellish state. The proper response to Satan's plan to labor "out of good still to find means of evil" is Adam's joyous cry when he has beheld the true turn of events:

O goodness infinite, goodness immense!
That all this good of evil shall produce,
And evil turn to good.
(XII. 469–71)

There is always a danger, of course, that one become over-ingenious in working out patterns such as those I have been describing. Yet the more one investigates the structural and syntactical surfaces of *Paradise Lost,* the more one recognizes the organic complexity of the epic. One thinks of the grand rhetorical passages that surge with energy only to return to a point from which they set out. Recall, for example, Belial's appeal against the advocates of continued war: "I should be much for open War," he feigns, "if what was urg'd/Main reason to persuade immediate War,/Did not dissuade me most." He then builds to the vivid depiction of the dimensions of the damned:

> wherefore cease we then?
> Say they who counsel War, we are decreed,
> Reserv'd and destin'd to Eternal woe;
> Whatever doing, what can we suffer more,
> What can we suffer worse? *is this then worst,*
> *Thus sitting, thus consulting, thus in Arms?*
> What when we fled amain, pursu'd and strook
> With Heav'n's afflicting Thunder, and besought
> The Deep to shelter us? this Hell then seem'd
> A refuge from those wounds: or when we lay
> Chain'd on the burning Lake? that sure was worse.
> What if the breath that kindl'd those grim fires
> Awak'd should blow them into sevenfold rage
> And plunge us in the flames? or from above
> Should intermitted vengeance arm again
> His red right hand to plague us? what if all
> Her stores were op'n'd, and this Firmament
> Of Hell should spout her Cataracts of Fire,
> Impendent horrors, threat'ning hideous fall
> One day upon our heads; while we perhaps
> Designing or exhorting glorious war,
> Caught in a fiery Tempest shall be hurl'd
> Each on his rock transfixt, the sport and prey
> Of racking whirlwinds, or for ever sunk
> Under yon boiling Ocean, *wrapt in Chains;*
> *There to converse with everlasting groans,*
> Unrespited, unpitied, unrepriev'd,
> Ages of hopeless end; *this would be worse.*
>   (II. 159–86; emphasis added)

The great tragic suspension of these lines from the question "is this then worst . . . ?" to the exhausted recognition of "this would be worse" frames the passage and makes dramatic what Christopher Ricks has called a sense of destiny rather than destination.[26] Within the frame of this question and answer, Belial opposes the idea of "consulting, thus in Arms" with the vision of conversing "wrapt in Chains," reinforcing the sense of circularity that underlies the entire passage.

Much more intricate in its antimetabolic organization, however, is the famous Vallombrosa image, which also employs suspension to create a sense of vast panoramic and historic tensions. The images describe Satan, "the superior Fiend," as he moves "toward the shore . . . Of that inflamed Sea" to stir his fallen legions:

> he stood and call'd
> His Legions, Angel Forms, who lay intrans't
> Thick as Autumnal Leaves that strow the Brooks
> In *Vallombrosa,* where th' *Etrurian* shades
> High overarch't imbow'r; or scatter'd sedge
> Afloat, when with fierce Winds *Orion* arm'd
> Hath vext the Red-Sea Coast, whose waves o'erthrew
> *Busiris* and his *Memphian* Chivalry,
> While with perfidious hatred they pursu'd
> The Sojourners of *Goshen,* who beheld
> From the safe shore thir floating Carcasses
> And broken Chariot Wheels; so thick bestrown
> Abject and lost lay these, covering the Flood,
> Under amazement of thir hideous change.
> He call'd so loud, that all the hollow Deep
> Of Hell resounded.
>
> (I. 300–315)

In this passage Milton moves inward from (1) a brief description of Hell's "inflamed sea," and (2) Satan's call (3) to his fallen legions (4) "who [5] lay [6] intrans't," (7) "Thick as Autumnal leaves that strow the Brooks/In Vallombrosa." At the center he offers us the image of exodus,

26. Ricks, p. 30.

an image that provides an emblem of God's providence in the midst of the circular description of the fallen Satanic horde, a historical, linear image of hope within the confines of apparent destruction. At this point, Milton moves outward from the center. The "broken Chariot Wheels" of the "Memphian Chivalry" bring us back to the fallen angels (7) "so thick bestrown" on the flood, (6) "Abject and lost [5] lay [4] these," (3) the hideously changed legions, (2) to whom Satan calls "so loud" that (1) "the hollow Deep/Of Hell resounded." With so much else happening in this passage, its structure remains absolutely unobstrusive and yet ever-present. Once again, Milton has made form consonant with meaning and both apposite to hope.

These large patterns may be reinforced by the prosodic rhythms of the poem as well. Studying the metrical texture of *Paradise Lost,* James Whaler points out that the more we analyze the "rhythmic ordonnance" of Milton's verse paragraph the clearer it is that his method is intentionally "analogous to that of contrapuntal music."[27] Whaler's investigations of the Miltonic paragraph later lead him to conclude that each of them is, "rhythmically, a finished

---

27. *Counterpoint and Symbol, Anglistica* 6 (Copenhagen, 1956): 16. James Whaler examines in elaborate detail the metrical and syntactical character of *Paradise Lost* and finds the poem to abound in polyphonic rhythms of beautiful symmetry and unbelievable complexity. Though one may feel that Whaler carries his analysis beyond the realm of the credible, it is difficult not to be impressed with his basic thesis, which establishes a persistent pattern of circular rhythms in metrical phrasing, based on the primary Pythagorean progressions, 1, 2, 3, 4, or 4, 3, 2, 1, such as the following:

> to him (1)
> Glory and praise, whose wisdom had ordain'd (2, 3)
> Good out of evil to create. (4)
> > (VII. 186–88)

> who reason for thir Law refuse, (4)
> Right reason for thir Law, and for thir King (3, 2)
> *Messiah.* (1)
> > (VI. 41–3)

contrapuntal piece" (p. 72). Whaler adduces an astounding amount of evidence that points to the conclusion that Milton consciously "fingered and computed the beats" again and again in key passages throughout the epic. Not only does such exactitude seem part of Milton's compositional method, but the fingering produces numerous passages that are rhythmically circular in much the way that the syntax and structure of the poem are circular. The following example from Whaler's study will illustrate the point. Investigating the 113-line verse paragraph in which Raphael describes the celestial motions to Adam (VIII. 66–178), Whaler discovers that the five-beat interval "What if the Sun/Be Centre to the World" begins at the center of the paragraph. Of the 565 beats in the paragraph, 283 precede Raphael's comment. In reference to this discovery, Whaler argues reasonably that in such a case involving "response not of symbolic number to content but merely of numerical reference in the context to location among beats, the odds against chance would seem overwhelming. If there were an abundance of 113-line paragraphs" with astronomical concerns we might expect some such thing to happen accidentally at some point, but this is the only paragraph of 113 lines in Milton's blank verse (pp. 82–83). Examination of the verbal structure of this verse paragraph lends support to Whaler's metrical contention and reveals much more about the interrelatedness of form and content in *Paradise Lost*.

The hypothetical statement about the sun's centrality is itself in the midst of seven lines, in which Raphael first explains that God "Placed Heav'n from Earth so far" precisely so that human sight would err and "no advantage gain" from astronomical speculation. Then Raphael turns to the astronomical hypothesis about the sun's position in the universe. From this hypothesis follows a complex statement of related hypotheses that continues for almost forty lines. By their very complexity these notions mirror the difficulties of astronomical debate and also draw us forward, providing a sense of psychological and temporal suspense necessary to the poet's ultimate meaning. Against the forward thrust, however, there is a larger, circular movement that may be likened to the circular dynamics of the universe itself. On either side of the central grouping of seven lines, that is, Milton contrives to present statements that mirror each other structurally and conceptually. The first such "ring" involves brief statements by Raphael —approximately five lines each—considering the difficulties man encounters when he seeks to distinguish between real and apparent motion in the heavens or with regard to the earth. On either side of these passages, Raphael discusses the generative mechanics of the universe, its size or scope, and the properties of speed with which it is endowed, a "Speed almost Spiritual," providing in terms of motion the counterpart to the "Maker's high magnificence" expressed by the vastness of his creation. The pertinence of these matters to Renaissance astronomy need hardly be emphasized. Of poetic and conceptual import in the two sections (lines 91–118 and 131–52), however, is the description of the generative properties of the universe, which insure that nothing is without purpose and that all engenders life. In the first section Raphael speaks of the interrelation between the virtue of the sun, which would "barren shine" and whose virtue would work no effect of itself unless received by "the fruitful Earth." Raphael makes much the same point in the later section in considering the light of the earth received by the moon and the possibility that

> other Suns perhaps
> With thir attendant Moons thou wilt descry
> Communicating Male and Female Light,
> Which two great Sexes animate the World.
> (VIII. 148–51)

Thus both passages have technical and conceptual matters in common concerning notions of proportion, motion, and purpose in the cosmic order of things.

Encircling them are two briefer statements (lines 85–91 and 153–58) by which Milton sharply marks off the true relevance of Raphael's remarks in connection with the astronomical debates of his own time. Raphael begins by indicating that he has noted in Adam's earlier attitude of inquiry a sense of bewilderment at the apparent "disproportion" in the vastness of the universe created merely to serve the needs of man on his tiny star. He returns to the point later and affirms that "such vast room in Nature unpossest" would surely lend itself to criticism. In essence, the concern over possible disproportion in the universe receives two separate explanations. Raphael first adduces a clear conceptualization: "Great or Bright infers not Excellence," emphasizing the obvious attributes of God and the mechanics of generation. When he comes back to the problem later, however, his discussion turns less on proofs than on the demands of faith. Here Raphael implies that for man to ponder "disproportion" argues a fault in creation, something one's faith in God cannot accept. The solution is indicative, it seems to me, of the way the entire argument is moving, from man's attempts at the mathematics or science of knowing to the firm reminder that faith offers the truer wisdom. The opening and closing lines of the verse paragraph elaborate the implications of this point with force and imagination.

But before considering those lines, I wish to discuss for a moment the relationship between the apparent structure of the verse paragraph and Milton's own sense of the structure of the universe. One might be tempted to read the central lines about the position of the sun in the universe as a veiled statement of Milton's "true" Copernican beliefs, opposed to the Aristotelian-Ptolemaic universe he creates poetically. In this case the overall organization of the paragraph, developing "Orb in Orb" toward a central point, would reinforce the scientific truth propounded by Copernicus and his followers. But I doubt that this is the case, even though there is evidence that Milton was sympathetic toward a great deal being advocated in the new astronomy and especially so in relation to the discoveries of Galileo. Despite these factors, it seems unlikely that he would have taken sides on the issue in *Paradise Lost.* As Allan H. Gilbert has said,

> Milton understood Galileo and applauded his studies, while at the same time using without hesitation the ideas of the older astronomy. And it would have been folly in Milton to have decided with certainty either for or against the Copernican view. Indeed, Huxley is credited with the remark that in his opinion the Ptolemaics of Galileo's time had rather the better of the argument. Until the publication of Newton's *Principia* in 1687, the Copernican system did not have an assured basis. To expect Milton to pass beyond interest in Galileo and consideration of his views as possible and probable, and definitely declare for Copernicus, is to ask him to do what only a professional astronomer had a right to do.[28]

Still, the passage clearly shows us an informed reader in matters astronomical. Gilbert indicates this, richly annotating the ways Raphael's discussion draws on Galileo's *Dialogo intorno ai due massimi sistemi del mondo tolemaico e copernicano* (1632) and is "an untechnical summary of his work by a master of compression who caught the spirit of that with which he dealt" (p. 163). But Gilbert stresses that Milton was not in any of his writings a defender of Galileo's discoveries. What he was concerned with, as most of his references to Galileo indicate, was his example as a champion of intellectual and scientific freedom against obscurantism. When Milton met Galileo under house arrest in Arcetri, he confronted an old man, embattled, perhaps em-

28. "Milton and Galileo," *SP* 19 (1922): 183–84.

bittered, still struggling to adjust to the loss of sight that had broken off his telescopic investigations of the moon, to which he had finally returned after the years of controversy with the Inquisition. And though Milton's vision of the universe was, no doubt, markedly affected by viewing its spaciousness and beauty through Galileo's telescope, as Marjorie Nicolson has suggested,[29] the really profound impression that he carried away from Arcetri was, I believe, of a different order. The strongest impressions seem to have been of the struggle that the aged astronomer had committed himself to with such an incredible vehemence and tenacity. For most of his mature life Galileo had been dominated by his desire to bring the Church to a truer knowledge of the facts of the physical universe as revealed through his telescope. When the struggle was finally over and the implications of defeat were fully evident, it was clear that the man of science had suffered as an advocate of reconciliation rather than as an apostle of the new astronomy.[30]

It was this impression, I believe, that stayed with Milton throughout the remainder of his life and charged his great poetry with those moments of what might be called a rebellious advocacy of truth. And though the tone and intensity are different, the same desire to bring the dicates of science and the higher wisdom into a meaningful coherence dominates Raphael's discussion, in statement and shape. The great astronomical hypothesis *remains* a hypothesis: "What if the Sun/Be Centre to the World" . . . "What if seventh to these [stars is] the planet Earth" . . . "What if that light," which shines from it, illuminates other worlds? However man finally regards these possibilities, it is his primary concern to see God in the shape of things: "Solicit not thy thoughts with matters hid," advises Raphael; "leave them

29. "Milton and the Telescope," *ELH* 2 (1935): 1–32.
30. See, for example, Ludovico Geymonat, *Galileo Galilei, A Biography and Inquiry into his Philosophy of Science*, trans. Stillman Drake (New York, 1965).

to God above, him serve and fear." And though this might well seem consonant with the arguments of the Church against Galileo, we would mistake Milton's true meaning if we stopped there. His argument moves irrevocably toward the final statement of joy in God's gifts:

> joy thou
> In what he gives to thee, this Paradise
> And thy fair *Eve:* Heav'n is for thee too high
> To know what passes there; be lowly wise:
> Think only what concerns thee and thy being;
> Dream not of other Worlds, what Creatures there
> Live, in what state, condition or degree,
> Contented that thus far hath been reveal'd
> Not of Earth only but of highest Heav'n.
> (VIII. 170–78)

Notions of time, place, and revelation are joined together in these final lines. With that conjunction we have, quite literally, come full circle. Raphael began his discussion saying:

> To ask or search I blame thee not, for Heav'n
> Is as the Book of God before thee set,
> Wherein to read his wond'rous Works, and learn
> His Seasons, Hours, or Days, or Months, or Years:
> This to attain, whether Heav'n move or Earth,
> Imports not, if thou reck'n right.
> (VIII. 66–71)

True wisdom knows its season. It is the knowledge of the time or season when all shall be revealed to those who have had the patience and faith to be, as Raphael says, "lowly wise" and who have thought only what concerns them and their being in time. The strong temporal emphasis marks the warning against all desire to feel "the future in the instant," the desire shortly to be acted upon in Eden in an attempt to annul time and gain from the future "other worlds" as yet undreamed of. Rather than a prohibition of any sort against curiosity and investigation, Milton provides a formula for discovery. As such, it is perfectly in line with Galileo's own statements in the *Dialogo*, which recognize the difficulties that face even the wisest man seeking to penetrate, at a specific moment in time, "i profondi abissi della sua infinita sapienza" and which stress the need to study the "gran libro della natura" in accordance with the "dottrina divina, . . . le maraviglie di Dio nel Cielo."[31] This is the true freedom to be gained in reading the Book of God. This is the reason for probing the beauty of the night sky. All things will be revealed in time, says the Angel, even as "thus far" it has been revealed. It is necessary merely to be patient and alert, and to have faith. The answers will be forthcoming as and when they are needed. But if, as some of Galileo's opponents refused to do, one will not look through the glass, all will remain dark.

The great astronomical passage in Book VIII of *Paradise Lost* may be likened to a flower, opening outward as it comes into bloom, revealing in the sunlight at the center the brilliance and mystery of truth.

As God prepares to send forth His Son to create the universe, Milton treats us to yet another circular passage, one that encompasses all time in a magnificent rhetorical period verbally imitative of the eternal process:

> I can repair
> That detriment, if such it be to *lose*
> *Self-lost,* and in a moment will create
> Another World, *out of one man a Race*
> *Of men innumerable,/there to dwell,*
> *Not here,* till by degrees of merit rais'd
> They open to themselves at length the way

31. Allan H. Gilbert, p. 183; *Dialogo*, etc., *Le Opere di Galileo Galilei* (Florence, 1842), 1:492,502,509–12.

Up hither, under long obedience tri'd,
And *Earth be chang'd to Heav'n,* and *Heav'n to Earth,*
One Kingdom, Joy and Union without end.
                    (VII. 152–61; emphasis added)

The whole passage turns on a vast temporal axis epito-
mized structurally in the penultimate line. In statement and
structure it fulfills the circular process of becoming and
leads into the final line, which provides a slow-moving pattern symbolic of the eternal stasis ultimately to be achieved
by man in God.

Rhetorically, as I have indicated, the previous quotations
provide examples of antimetable, the repetition of words
or ideas in inverse order. As a rhetorical pattern, antimetabole is, under the designation of "hysteron proteron," one of the devices recommended to the preacher by
Erasmus and Keckermann, as a figure to be found in the
Bible and employed by the Church Fathers. Milton was, no
doubt, familiar with the tradition and the example usually
cited from the opening of John: "In principio erat verbum,
et verbum erat apud Deum, et Deus erat verbum"—a figure
expressive of the unending relationship between God and
the Word of Creation. Of several examples from Augustine, the closing lines of *De Civitate Dei* XIX, 27, provide a
good example of the circular style:

> Et hoc illic in omnibus atque in singulis aeternum erit aeter-
> numque esse certum erit, et ideo pax beatitudinis huius vel
> beatitudo pacis huius summum bonum erit.

Examples of this preacher's device can also be found in
Donne's sermons. Admonishing his auditors, Donne reminds them of "those men that died in their sins, that
sinned in their dying" and warns that man is delivered over
"to punishment for sinne, and to sin for punishment."[32]

32. See *D. Erasmi . . . Ecclesiastae sive de ratione concionandi libri quatuor* (Basil. 1535);
also Keckermann's *Rhetoricae Ecclesiasticae . . .* 3rd ed. (Hanover, 1606). Thomas
Granger, *Syntagma Logicum, or the Divine Logike. Serving especially for the use of Divines*

Herbert Austin has indicated that for Dante such chiasmic patterns amounted to an obsession in his attempts—culminating in the complete spiritual vision of *Paradiso* XXX. 46–96—to depict "the immaterial reverse of all things." Discussing Dante's description of the marble relief of the Annunciation in *Purgatorio* X, Austin shows how "as a result of the Angelic greeting *'Ave,'* Mary, on her side, was enabled to undo, that is *reverse,* what had been done to humanity's hurt by disobedient *Eva,* the letters of whose name are the reverse of that *'Ave.'* " Suggesting a relationship between the reversing processes of Egyptian hieroglyphics, the Greek "boustrephedon," and various magical acts "by which evil could be achieved by reversing good utterances," Austin indicates that Dante employs

> the general phenomena and concepts of reflection, reversed direction, and geometrical introversion of retroversion to an extraordinary extent, in his *Divine Comedy,* to indicate the opposition and the salutary undoing-effect of the Spiritual World with regard to the world of base matter.[33]

It is just such a purpose, of course, that would recommend the reflexive word-pattern to Milton, and with the prece-

---

in the practise of preaching (1620), p. 318, and William Lisle, *A Saxon Treatise concerning the Old and New Testament,* etc., (1623), p. 15, justify the use of the device, which they term "hysterosis," by the preacher and religious writer. In particular, Lisle is defending the use of the device by AElfric. For a discussion of the figure in relation to epic writing see Cedric Whitman, *Homer and the Heroic Tradition* (Cambridge, Mass., 1958), chaps. 5 and 11. For the lines from Donne see *The Sermons,* ed. Simpson and Porter (Berkeley, 1953), VI. No. 18, 1. 394 and VII. No. 2, 11. 235–36.

33. Herbert Austin's essays on Dante are "From Matter to Spirit," *MLN* 38 (1923): 140–48 and "The Arrangement of Dante's Purgatorial Reliefs," *PMLA* 47 (1932): 1–9. The circular style has been discussed by Leo Spitzer in a review of *Le Haut Livre du Graal: Perlesvaus,* ed. W. A. Nitze and others (Chicago, 1938), *MLN* 53 (1938): 604–6, and in "Le Style 'Circulaire,' " *MLN* 55 (1940): 495–99. Austin's work provides brilliant analyses of Dante's use of the circular style and its relation to pictorial as well as mystical effects. Spitzer refers to Hans Leisegang's *Denkformen* (1928), a study of the broad persistence of the circular style in mannerist writing, which relates that style, among other things, to mystical writing. Georges Poulet considers the circular style in passing in his *Métamorphoses du cercle,* cited above.

dent of sacred writing before him, Milton could be expected to embrace this sign of the divine rhetoric.

Related to his use of the figure of antimetabole is Milton's habit of encircling one word with two others that syntactically depend upon it, a habit that further emphasizes the circular motif of his poem. The technique has normally been explained as an element in Milton's Latinizing of the language,[34] one of the numerous ways he sought to dignify his diction and lend it a Virgilian cast. No doubt this is so. But the pattern has a rhythm and persistence so pronounced in relation to the overall significance of the poem, that Milton may well have been employing the syntactical device as something of what we would term a "subliminal" reminder of the organic nature of all things.[35] From the many examples of the technique present in *Paradise Lost,* a few may suffice to illustrate the circular rhythm established in the pattern. At the outset of the poem, as I have said earlier, Milton describes the creative spirit, which "with mighty wings outspread/*Dove-like satst brooding* on the vast Abyss" (I. 20–21; here and below the emphasis is added). Satan recognizes that *"long* is *the way/*And *hard"* that leads out of Hell (II. 432–33). In his quest upward into the light he flies through "dun Air sublime" (III. 72), but unlike the future state of man through God's mercy, Satan remains *"dead* in *sins* and *lost"* (III. 233). He will never be able to renew himself as can Adam and Eve, who daily

34. See Raymond Dexter Havens, *The Influence of Milton on English Poetry* (Cambridge, Mass., 1922), pp. 80–81.
35. Even Milton's use of the pun may be basic to the energy of the poem. Ricks, who has carefully studied the function of word-play in *Paradise Lost* (*Milton's Grand Style*) indicates how Milton's interest in etymological puns was related to classical-biblical traditions, which held that etymology was intimately connected with the true nature of the thing itself. The use of word-play in the seventeenth century was a serious thing, for in the pun was to be found evidence of God's wit and wisdom in the vast network of correspondences He had established throughout the universe. Creation was like a giant poem, rich in metaphor and correspondences. The pun, then, was less a verbal embarrassment in serious hands than it was a mark of the relationships, more or less hidden, which upon discovery told us more about God's truth and the richness of Creation.

through prayer *"Firm peace recovr'd* and *wonted calm"* (V. 210).[36] Such patterns, I believe, are basic to the creative energy of *Paradise Lost.* Throughout his epic Milton reinforces the primary tension between good and evil in narrative and imagistic terms by organic verbal patterns such as those I have just discussed. Concerning the great structural design of *Paradise Lost* I have still to speak, but I hope at this point to have provided sufficient examples of the verbal mannerisms of *Paradise Lost* to support my claim that Milton employs a large number of verbal devices to echo on a mystical level the great creative theme of renewal that lies at the heart of his poem. Noting Milton's pronounced reliance on oxymoron in the opening books of the epic, John Peter says:

> Such collocations take their life from the tension between the syntax and meaning. So far as meaning goes words like "visible," "ruin'd," "precious," etc., tend naturally to fly off from the nouns and verbs they are made to modify, but syntax restrains them, tethering them in place. The effect is that a sort of vibrancy is set up within the phrase.[37]

Peter's description of the interaction between syntax and meaning in oxymoron serves, I believe, to define the overall verbal energy and rhythm latent in *Paradise Lost.* In the oxymoronic pattern there is a centripetal force at work, which suggests not only the divine plan but something of the grimness of the divine humor, as well. Positively, the divine activity manifests itself in the related force of paradox. The fallen angels endure a living death. Their situation is that "life dies, death lives"; the hopelessness of the personification subsumes paradox. For man, however, the

36. Though other examples of this well-known syntactical device need hardly be adduced, a few more ready to hand are: "so thick a drop serene" (III. 25); "Temperate vapours Bland" (V. 5); "gather'd aught of evil, or conceal'd" (V. 207); "Unvoyageable gulf obscure" (X. 366); and "heavenly form/Angelic" (IX. 457–58).

37. *A Critique of Paradise Lost* (New York, 1960), p. 39.

struggle to overcome evil will, if successful, reverse the apparent truth of death. Paradox shows him that out of loss will come gain, whereas Satan's gains are only losses, a "precious bane" for the "Archangel ruin'd." The central paradox of *Paradise Lost,* the fortunate Fall, is itself, in one sense, the Hellish oxymoron turned round as a result of man's faith in God's wisdom and grace. Throughout *Paradise Lost,* then, Milton creates a style that physically as well as intuitively *reflects* the re-creative powers, the renewal that symbolizes the divine abundance of creation.

2

His Circle Drawn Just

Turning from rhetorical aspects of *Paradise Lost,* I wish to examine the ways in which the poem's physical structure provides the primary manifestation of its circular design. As I mentioned, I believe Milton designed his epic as a concrete, though mystical, sign of God's wisdom, as a hieroglyph of the unending providence that sustains man in time. The details of syntax and image provide numerous small intimations of the scheme, like Wordsworth's "shadowy recollections" which "are yet the fountain light of all our day." The larger structural design establishes the shape "of that immortal sea." To change the allusion, one might compare the interrelationship between detail and general design achieved by Milton with the method of *Walden.* In that book the enigmatic details Thoreau asks us to ponder often turn out to epitomize the cyclical framework of the whole, a framework that defines through the shape of the year the metaphysical sense that "the sun is but a morning star."

Throughout *Paradise Lost* Milton creates a structural frame, like a vast antimetabole, in which passage after passage finds its narrative or thematic counterpart reflected across the surface of the poem. The entire design moves

toward the central image of Christ's victory over Satan
during the rebellion in Heaven, an event symbolic of the
eternal victory of good over evil. Thus, in effect, the design
reinforces or complements both the concentric structure of
the Miltonic universe and the traditional image of God
Himself:

> from Him all things did flow and spring, namely out of a secret
> and hidden nature to a revealed and manifest condition, from
> an unknown estate unto an evident and known existence; from a
> pure archetypal simplicity into a real type of similitude; from a
> radical fountain into a sea, and from a mere point into a circle or
> circumference; verifying that saying of the wise philosopher:
> God is the center of everything, whose circumference is no-
> where to be found; that is, in all and beyond all.

This is Robert Fludd in his *Mosaical Philosophy.*[1] Others
employ the image of a stone thrown into the water genera-
ting circular ripples ever expanding from the center of
impact to designate the nature of God and his continual
creative force.[2] Similar concepts no doubt lie behind Milton's description of the arrangement of the angelic hosts
around God:

> Thus when in Orbs
> Of circuit inexpressible they stood,
> Orb within Orb, the Father infinite,
> By whom in bliss imbosom'd sat the Son,
> Amidst as from a flaming Mount, whose top
> Brightness had made invisible.
> (V. 594–99)

They also influence the ironic image of the broken pattern
of Hell where the demons listening to Satan bend

---

1. (London, 1659), pp. 133–34. Fludd's "wise philosopher" is Hermes Trismegis-
tus.
2. See Georges Poulet, *Les Métamorphoses du cercle*, pp. 9–10.

> thir doubl'd Ranks . . .
> From wing to wing, and half enclose him round
> With all his Peers.
>
> (I. 616–18)

The basic design of *Paradise Lost* is similar to that which Cedric Whitman has described in relation to the *Iliad*. One can say of Milton, as Whitman said of Homer, that the poet creates a "circular composition" of "scenes framing scenes in concentric rings around centerpieces, exactly as central motifs are heavily framed by borders in Geometric painting." Rhetorically, Whitman relates this kind of structure to the device of "hysteron proteron" which like "ring composition . . . returns to its point of origin and effects circularity of design." More recently, Brooks Otis has ably demonstrated that similar patterns of recessed symmetry are present both in the *Aeneid* and in Virgil's *Eclogues* and *Georgics*.[3] Milton also thus organizes complete books in balanced but inverse patterns. The scheme is so carefully worked out by Milton, as I will endeavor to show, that in its entirety it presents a consistent circular composition that can be schematically represented—substituting letters for the numerical designations of the twelve books:

A B C D E F : F E D C B A

Now, clearly, there are arguments that may be advanced against an over-hasty acceptance of this thesis. For one, it

---

3. *Homer and the Heroic Tradition* (Cambridge, Mass., 1958). pp. 97, 254. Whitman cites S. E. Bassett, *The Poetry of Homer*, Sather Classical Lectures, vol. 15 (Berkeley, Calif., 1958), pp. 119 ff. as his authority on classical notions of circular compositions in Homer from Aristarchus forward. Of particular interest beyond the classical concerns is Bassett's recapitulation of biblical scholarship, which has demonstrated that "early Hebrew literature abounds in the Homeric hysteron proteron." The form is not simply "confined to poetry; it is found in the unstudied utterances of Jesus and . . . in simple historical statements in the more primitive books of the Old Testament. . . . Apparently, no matter how much Hebrew poets used the inverted order to give form to their couplets and larger architectural units, the tendency to inversion is inherent in the ancient Hebrew speech and literature." Brooks Otis's *Virgil: A Study in Civilized Poetry* (Oxford, 1964), provides a wealth of speculative detail on symmetrical structure in Virgil's poetry. For the *Aeneid*, one should consult chapters VI and VII, on the "Odyssean" and "Iliadic" *Aeneid*, respectively.

will be evident in a poem as long and complex as *Paradise Lost* that examples of passages that do not have counterparts will far outnumber those that do. But this hardly seems to deny the large pattern. Surely it would be extremely unlikely for even a majority of passages to match each other in this way. The greater the number of "mirror" images within the poem, the greater the danger of the poem's degenerating into a purely mechanical exercise. Still, the number of matched scenes or passages in *Paradise Lost* is sufficient to make the pattern clear though never obtrusive. It is a measure of Milton's skill and daring as an artist that he could work with such a pattern and not overwork it.

It is important to remember, beyond this, that the reflexive pattern represents but one of many elements in the overall design of Milton's work. It signifies the mystical level of his conception. Other tensions remain. Other patterns exist to define them in the total orchestration of the epic. Acceptance of the notion of a reflexive pattern, however, involves the necessity of describing a work created in a temporal medium by means of a spatial metaphor. Writing about aspects of the theory of fiction, Frank Kermode reminds us that "forms in space . . . have more temporality than Lessing supposed, since we have to read them in sequence before we can know they are there, and the relations between them."[4] Kermode admits that this is less true of poems than of prose fiction, but his observation remains central to any analysis of what we mean when we discuss the design or "shape" of *Paradise Lost*. Yet, though the metaphoric force of spatial terminology will always persist to some extent in speaking of a work of prose or poetry, in the case of *Paradise Lost* the metaphoric quality of the terms is minimal. Various strong aesthetic habits of mind lay behind the seventeenth-century poet's feeling for the spatial nature of his work. In discussing proportion in poetry, for

4. *The Sense of an Ending,* pp. 178–79.

example, George Puttenham spoke of the relationships between "the arithmetical, the geometrical, and the musical"
aspects of verse, and went on to employ the shaped poem,
poemata figurata, as illustrative of "geometrical proportion."[5] Figured verse was a manifestation of geometrical
proportion related both to Renaissance interest in the classical concept of *ut pictura poesis* and to the religio-symbolic
tendency of seeing the emblems of God spread throughout
the universe. On the lowest level, the shaped poem was
visually and poetically a mannerist trifle with antecendents
at least as far back as Simmias. But handled in a more
sophisticated way, it could create links between the visual
and verbal fields of perception that emphasized the oneness
of the material and spiritual essence. The shaped poem
represented, as Joseph Summers has demonstrated in discussing the poetry of George Herbert,

> a fusion of the spiritual and material, of the rational and sensu-
> ous, in the essential terms of formal relationships . . . The
> hieroglyphs, whether of God's or of man's creation, were to be
> "read" rather than adored, and they sent the reader back to
> God.[6]

5. *The Arte of English Poesie,* ed. Gladys D. Willcock and Alice Walker (Cambridge,
1936), pp. 64 and 91ff. It is particularly interesting to note Puttenham's description (pp. 98–99) of the "round":

> The most excellent of all figures geometrical is the round for its many perfec-
> tions . . . First because he is even and smooth, without any angle, or interruption,
> most voluble and apt to turn and to continue motion, which is the author of life.
> He containeth in him the commodious description of every other figure, and for
> his ample capacity doth resemble the world or universe, and for his indefinite-
> ness, having no special place of beginning or end, beareth a similitude with God
> and eternity.

After speaking of the "principal parts" of the figure: the circle, itself, its center,
and its beam, or radius, Puttenham introduces one of his own poems by way of
illustration, rhyming at the beginning and ending thus: A B C D—D C B A. The
poem's subject is God's eternal round. The whole section provides a minor
illustration of the kind of structural principle I am investigating in relation to
Paradise Lost.
6. *George Herbert: His Religion and Art* (London, 1954), p. 146.

Now, of course, Milton's epic is not a shaped poem in the formal sense that Herbert's *Altar* or *Easter Wings* are figure poems, but Milton conceived it spatially, I believe, as a hieroglyph of the universal order of things. And though we may not be able to "perceive" the entire structure until we have finished reading, Milton has so fashioned the poem that we may sense its design intuitively. In this, too, he may be imitating the universal scheme. For, clearly, it is not given to man to know the total design of things until the poetry of his life is complete. Renaissance notions about perception and psychology allow for an intuitive awareness of design. For example, belief in the perfect mathematics and harmonious structure of the universe, of which man's soul is naturally a part, gave rise to the conviction in architecture, as Rudolf Wittkower has shown, that "if a church has been built in accordance with essential mathematical harmonies, we react instinctively." It is as if "an inner sense tells us without rational analysis, that we perceive an image of the vital force behind all matter—of God Himself."[7]

The assumptions of this chapter necessarily include the proposition that the final form of *Paradise Lost* resulted from a desire on Milton's part to perfect the overall structure of his epic. Without new evidence, we will probably never be able to say definitely whether Milton reorganized *Paradise Lost* from ten to twelve books with a particular artistic purpose in mind, or whether the changes were forced upon him by the relatively trivial needs of printer and publisher. It is my belief, however, that the changes, slight but not insignificant, suit with the general design of

7. *Architectural Principles of the Age of Humanism* (London, 1952), p. 25. Susanne K. Langer's *Mind: An Essay on Human Feeling* (Baltimore, 1967), vol. 1, provides much theoretical support for the idea that the structure of the whole of a work that has been organically patterned may be perceived in and through its parts. Her analysis of "Living Form in Art and Nature," pp. 199–244, is particularly illuminating.

the epic that I am describing. Along with Arthur Barker, I feel that the changes undertaken in the second edition of *Paradise Lost* represent "Milton's last recorded comment on his poem."[8]

The revisions made in *Paradise Lost*—apart from changes in spelling and punctuation—were relatively few. Those that concern us at present are the structural and textual changes resulting from the reorganization of the poem from ten to twelve books. To accomplish the reorganization, Milton divided the original books seven and ten into the present seven and eight, and eleven and twelve, respectively. Thus the former eighth and ninth books had to be renumbered nine and ten. Broadly considered, the reorganization allowed certain aspects of the poem's circular construction to be more clearly articulated. Whereas the exact linear middle of the poem remained virtually unchanged,[9] the redivision into twelve books emphasized the midpoint of the poem's overall structure by matching the six books of the first half of the poem with six in the second half. Though Milton had written at the opening of Book VII that half his poem "yet remains unsung," obviously the old book division did not make this claim apparent:

I, II, III, IV, V, VI——VII, VIII, IX, X

Thematically, the change allows Milton to emphasize the dichotomy between destruction and creation. As Joseph Summers has ponted out in *The Muse's Method*, in the first edition of *Paradise Lost*

---

8. "Structural Pattern in *Paradise Lost*," p. 19.
9. The middle of the first edition comes at VI.761–62 as Messiah ascends His chariot in preparation for His attack on Satan and the rebellious angels. Though the new center (VI. 766) is part of the same description, it obscures the emphasis on light and elevation that Milton achieved in the first edition of the poem. Gunnar Qvarnstrom discusses the position and the numerological symbolism of the "central elevation scene" in detail in *The Enchanted Palace* (Stockholm, 1967), pp. 55ff. Alastair Fowler's *Triumphal Forms: Structural Patterns in Elizabethan Poetry* (Cambridge, 1970) follows Qvarnstrom but considers the thematic implications of the "sovereign triumph" at the center of Milton's epic (see pp. 116ff.).

the actions of the angel Abdiel, bridging the end of Book V and the beginning of Book VI, are at the center of the poem . . . Abdiel remains of the utmost importance in the final version. The significance of his action remains, but the emphasis has changed; for in the final version the War in Heaven and the Creation of the world are clearly at the center. Milton seems to have discovered that in the poem which he had written the true center was not the angelic exemplum of man's ways at their most heroic, but the divine image of God's ways at their most providential. (pp. 112–13)

In this regard, it is worth noting that the new emphasis on the center, both thematically and structurally, finds precedence in other works that Milton knew, though whether he reconized their structural emphasis can not be said.

Among works whose center seems to have particular, even esoteric significance, one might begin with the *Republic* of Plato. It has long been argued that the center of the *Republic* presents the main thesis of the work. Having outlined his idealistic program, Socrates is questioned on the means of implementing the scheme. His answer is striking in statement and structure: Ἐὰν μή, . . . ἤ οἱ φιλόσοφοι βασιλεύσωσιν ἐν ταῖς πόλεσιν ἤ οἱ βασιλεις τε νῦν λεγόμενοι καὶ δυνάσται φιλοσοφήσωσι . . . "Unless . . . the philosophers rule as kings or those now called kings and chiefs genuinely and adequately philosophize . . .," the plan can not be brought into being. The rhetorical pattern of the answer mirrors the intellectual process of the book, which works toward the center of things and then back out from them. The central reference to the means of triumphant sovereignty is particularly provocative in light of Alastair Fowler's recent study of this image as it came down to and was embraced by Renaissance arts. Fowler adduces numerous examples of works that have been designed so that they reveal at their center an image of sovereign triumph, of "the Lord in the midst of the earth" (Exod. 8:22). Though many of his examples come from Renaissance

trionfi and related Elizabethan works, his scope includes a
host of authors from Virgil to the English Augustans. Two
other works of particular significance in relation to *Paradise
Lost* are the *Aeneid* and *Commedia*. The midpoint in the
Aeneid carries something of the same thematic weight as
that of *Paradise Lost*. As others have shown, Aeneas goes
into the underworld a Trojan and returns a Latin. He
emerges from Hades at the end of Book Six changed, transformed in mind and purpose. At the beginning of Book
Seven he reaches the shores of Latium. Turning to Dante's
Commedia, I would cite Charles Singleton's recent study of
"The Poet's Number at the Center," in which he shows that
the "central pivot of the whole poem in terms of the action,
in terms, that is, of what happens to the wayfarer Dante as
he 'passes through the center' " comes in the exact center
of the seventeenth canto of the *Purgatorio* and defines "the
general exposition of Love, which is shown to be the all-
embracing and all-motivating force of creatures and Creator." Of course, even these several instances do not make
a tradition, and there is little beyond internal evidence to
support the theory that a tradition did, in fact, exist, to be
handed down from poet to poet. But the obvious percep-
tual and symbolic significance of the center in any work of
art remains for all to see and weigh.[10]

The new distribution of books in *Paradise Lost* also clarified a number of particular correspondences or interrelationships between the two halves of the poem. The rela-

10. See the *Republic of Plato*, trans. Allan Bloom (New York, 1968), V. 473d, p.
153. Alastair Fowler, in *Triumphal Forms*, discusses, among others, examples from
Virgil, Horace, Dante, Chaucer, Spenser, Marvell, and Milton. For the structural
pattern at the center of the *Aeneid*, see Brooks Otis, *Virgil: A Study of Civilized Poetry*.
Singleton's essay on Dante is in *MLN* 80 (1965): 1–10. Leo Strauss has long
shown an interest in esoteric writing of this kind. See especially his essay on Moses
ben Maimon in *Persecution and the Art of Writing* (Glencoe, Ill., 1952). If one were
to pursue the question of the significance of the center, other works that might
prove interesting to investigate are Machiavelli's *The Prince*, Montaigne's *Essays*,
and several of Shakespeare's later plays. A colleague of mine, Ronald Sharp, has
also pointed to the center of Shelley's *Defense of Poetry*, as having especial interest
in this regard.

tionship between the two Edenic books—formerly IV and VIII—provides a good example of this. In the first edition the positioning of the books in relation to each other is asymmetrical rather than balanced:

—, —, —, IV, —, —, —, VIII, —, —.

In the second, the books stand opposite each other in the same relative position:

—, —, —, IV, —, —, —, —, IX, —, —, —.

Just so, the division of Book X into XI and XII allowed the "historical" nature of those books about fallen man to be seen in comparison with that of the opening two books about the fallen angels. There are also numerological aspects that redistribution manifested, which I shall discuss in a moment. Generally, as Barker says, however, the revisions

> shift the poem's emphasis and its center in a way that would point more clearly to its stated intention. *Paradise Lost* was always meant to be a poem whose beginning is disobedience, whose middle is woe, and whose ultimate end is restoration. It may be that the intention was clouded in 1667, or that Milton's view of restoration was obscured. The 1674 revision is at any rate an effort to clarify the poem's ways.[11]

In arguing *for* the value of the ten-book structure, John Shawcross remarks apropos of Barker's position that though

> the epic form which the poem had taken on called for twelve books and emphasis on the triad of disobedience, woe, and restoration . . . Milton had certainly decided well before 1665 (when the manuscript was apparently complete) to turn his dramatic attempts into epic, and the suggested triad is not taken up in any such organized order in the work. The redistribution may emphasize the Son's example for those who look only at things symmetrical as having balance, but this does not

11. "Structural Pattern in *Paradise Lost*," p. 28.

mean that such symmetry was necessary for Milton or even entirely desirable in the poem.[12]

I admit to being one of those who tend to look "at things symmetrical as having balance." What I find most disturbing about Shawcross's argument at this point, however, is his reversal of matters to support his inference. It would seem more reasonable, that is, to adduce the changes brought about by the redistribution as evidence of Milton's aesthetic point of view rather than as evidence of the opposite. And, indeed, much of Milton's earlier poetry attests to a strong habit of mind that does think of things in terms of balanced opposites.

To accomplish the redivision of *Paradise Lost*, Milton added three lines to the beginning of what is now Book VIII and five lines to the beginning of Book XII. These can be called essential additions. Distinguished from them are

12. "The Balanced Structure of *Paradise Lost*," p. 711. James Whaler's point of view in *Counterpoint and Symbol* is almost the opposite of that of Shawcross. Whaler believes that the

> division into ten books in 1667 is all prepared to shift to a division into twelve. . . . Milton must indeed have some very peculiar, very private reason for issuing this work in a manner that seems in Ed. 1 to outrage one of the instincts of his nature—right proportioning.
>   But his indulgence in numerical symbol introduces us here to a rival, though subsurface, concept of proportioning. Mere division into books is not the only actuating motive. The presence of symbol within the books, within the paragraphs, sheds more than a ray of light across the grand partitioning of Ed. 1. . . . *The division of Ed. 1 is meant to effect a descending primary Pythagorean progression by the thematic groupings of its successive books.* Its directional significance is unmistakable. It is consistent with the identical retrograde series 4, 3, 2, 1, scattered through the rhythms of *Paradise Lost,* where it always responds to contextual situations involving disaster, defeat, moral obliquity, loss, sorrow. . . .
>   Numerical symbol therefore explains the *temporary* partitioning of Ed. 1. . . . The division of 1667 is temporary tribute to his Muse by way of Pythagorean symbol; that of 1674 is permanent tribute to epic tradition and its most inspired exemplar. (pp. 164–65)

While I am in sympathy with much that Whaler says about *Paradise Lost* and am deeply impressed with his findings, discussed earlier, I feel that his explanation of Milton's "temporary tribute" is unacceptable for it involves a structure in the descending progression that implies not justification but, as he says, "disaster, defeat, moral obliquity, loss. . . ."

three other changes, which added seven lines in Books V
and XI: V. 636–40—expanded from two lines in the first
edition; XI. 485–87—three lines added to the catalogue of
ways man will meet death in the postlapsarian world; and
XI. 551–52—expanded from a single line in the first edition. None of these changes is vital to the redivision. All
may be described in this context therefore as random or
nonessential additions. For this very reason, Milton's mo-
tive in adding the lines should be carefully considered. My
own guess is that the lines have no intrinsic value. I find it
difficult to explain them as substantive changes except as
they may be meant to provide an additional number of lines
that would bring the new total in the poem to a numerologically symbolic sum. The second edition of twelve books is
10,565 (not 10,558) lines long, fifteen lines having been
added to the original 10,550 lines of the first edition, which
number, as Shawcross says, seems to exemplify the Pythagorean "perfect number ten in various ways." Shawcross adds that to "Pythagoras ten indicated completeness,
the total of all things; it and its multiplicity returned to
unity" (p. 708). Precedent for the use of the number ten
and its multiples for structurally symbolic purposes can be
found, of course, in Dante's *Commedia*. But I would note
that the sense of "completeness, the total of all things"
represented by the number ten would not be fully appropriate to Milton's final vision. Though *Paradise Lost* embraces all time—indeed, eternity—its primary concept relates to regeneration, to the epiphanic vision of the future
possibilities that confront man and Milton. *Paradise Lost*
shared with the *Aeneid,* as the Renaissance read the latter's
allegorical meaning,[13] the sense of a new beginning rather

13. Renaissance critics had commented on what they felt was the symbolic significance of the twelve-book design of the *Aeneid* (see R. M. Cummings, "Two
Sixteenth-Century Notices of Numerical Composition in Virgil's *Aeneid,*" *N&Q*
16, n.s. (1969): 26–27), and it was early felt that Milton's reason for changing to
the twelve-book structure resulted from his desire to follow Virgil (see Tickell's
Spectator paper #632 (13 December 1714).

than of a closing off of things. The twelve-book format gains in relation to the Christian sense both of the number three now present in the overall pattern and of twelve, often seen to signify faith in the Trinity's permeating the four parts of the earth. The new line total preserves something of the idea of perfection yet adds the significant integer six, the first perfect number, symbolic of that *earthly* perfection that the poem seeks to exemplify, a perfection to be realized only in the future in the being of Christ made man. Six was thus the number by which to measure mortals, the number ultimately equated with the soul. Through the hexameral tradition, of course, six was also related to the creation and therefore, we may suppose, a logical unit by which to structure the second half of the poem, setting the six books of God's creative ways against the first six books, which broadly describe Satan's destructive program.

All the preceding speculation would be totally unwarranted if it were not for a number of factors in *Paradise Lost* that seem to suggest an interest on Milton's part in numerology as a structural element in his poem, an interest fostered, no doubt, by the notions that number lay behind the actual structure of the universe and that knowledge of its mystical signs revealed to the initiate the pattern of the cosmos.[14]

14. The mechanics of number symbolism are much too varied and complicated to survey here. Precedence for arithmetical exegesis of the Bible, especially for those passages which in literal interpretation seemed meaningless, lay in such Old Testament writings as the description of the Ark and Tabernacle and, specifically, in the statement in the *Wisdom of Solomon* (11:21): "Omnia in measura, et numero, et pondere disposiusti" ("All things in number, measure, and weight have been ordered"). It is interesting, in passing, to recall that Andrew Marvell ended his poem on *Paradise Lost* with a direct reference to Milton's having composed his poem in these terms:

> I too transported by the mode offend,
> And while I meant to *praise* thee, must *commend*.
> Thy verse created like thy theme sublime,
> In Number, Weight, and Measure, needs not rhyme.

Numerological theology was not adopted by early Christianity. What symbolism there was relating to biblical criticism persisted from Hebraic writings on the Old Testament. It was not until the third century that numerological investigation of

In *Paradise Lost* it appears to me that the changes made in the second edition of the epic suggest certain numerical readings that are consonant with the complexity of the *architectonicé* of the epic that I am endeavoring to describe. In settling for a twelve-book structure in place of the original ten books, Milton seems to shift his emphasis from Pythagorean to Christian numerology. In place of the closed perfection of the number 10, he introduces in the number 12, as I have said, the circular vision that opens the way to God.

Though it is easy to overdo the investigation of arithmetical aspects in *Paradise Lost*,[15] a few of the relationships present from the beginning or clarified by the redivision of the second edition require careful consideration. First of all, redivision produces a clearer conjunction between the description of the Creation and its location in the design of the poem. Seven is the number of creation. Whereas, in the old form of the epic, seven was the book that took up the

the New Testament became pronounced. Those who did most among the early Church Fathers to establish the importance of numerological exegesis of the Bible were Clement, Origen, Hippolytus, Augustine, and Cassiodorus. But it was Augustine, in particular, fascinated by the significance of numbers in relation to the hidden meanings of the Divine Wisdom, who was most important in fostering the Church's concern in the arcane art. Milton's great interest in Augustine's writings suggests that the poet would have read those of his passages which were strongly numerological with a sympathetic eye. This in itself, however, would not support the thesis that Milton was thereby prompted to practice numerical composition in his poetry. Though there is no external evidence that numerical composition interested Milton, it is worth noting that Milton's first mathematics teacher, Alexander Gil, the elder, had mathematical interests that are "discernible in the numerology of his cabbalistic citations and quotations." (Fletcher Harris, *The Intellectual Development of John Milton* (Urbana, Ill. 1956), 1: 357). For a concise introduction to the subject of numerology, see Vincent Foster Hopper, *Medieval Number Symbolism* (New York, 1938). Fowler, *Triumphal Forms*, provides a useful critical defense of the method in his introductory chapter.

15. Many studies of late have investigated numerological elements in Renaissance literature. Among the most important for Milton scholars are Gunnar Qvarnström, Alastair Fowler, and Maren-Sofie Røstvig, *The Hidden Sense: Milton and the Neoplatonic Method of Numerical Composition* (Oslo, 1963). Important statements in the developing discussion of numerology are C. A. Patrides, "The Numerological Approach to Cosmic Order during the English Renaissance," *ISIS*, 49 (1958): 391–97, A. Kent Hieatt's *Short Time's Endless Monument. The Symbolism of the Numbers in Edmund Spenser's Epithalamion* (New York, 1960), and Alastair Fowler's *Spenser and the Numbers of Time* (London, 1965), an analysis of the *Faerie Queene*.

Creation of the universe, it took up much more as well, including Adam's discussion with Raphael of the celestial motions, his recollection of his own creation, and Raphael's description of angelic love. Also in the revised edition, Book X becomes the location of man's decision to pray for salvation after his fall and of God's willingness to forgive. Here Milton sets God's perfect plan, as symbolized in the perfect number ten, in proper relation to Satan's imperfect victory, symbolized in the number nine, which means defect within perfection. Book XI chronicles the ages of sin leading up to the Flood, and eleven was known as the number of sin. Thus the promise of a new nation sprung from the seed of Abraham and the coming of the Messiah are the subjects appropriate to Book XII, the numerical designation of which signified faith in the Trinity suffused throughout the world.

Redivision also sets Books IV and IX in direct relationship, schematically as well as thematically. These are the edenic books, and in terms of Christian numerology their number designations were the basic integers of the mundane sphere. As a result of the analogies with the four elements, seasons, winds, rivers, the number four became associated specifically with the mundane. While the first three days of the Creation were said to adumbrate the trinity, the fourth was the "type of man." Man was a tetrad, a fact mystically understood in the name Adam, whose letters were the four winds.[16] The number nine signified defect within perfection. But it also related to the operation of the first cause on earth. It was in this sense that Dante described Beatrice, who was a nine, as a miracle.[17] Ironically, nine is both the perfect form of three, its square root, and thus the number of God, and also associated with the Devil through the Old Testament figure of King Og, who

16. Hopper, p. 84; cf. Augustine, *On John*, IX, 14.
17. Hopper, pp. 138–39; see *La Vita Nuova*, XXX, 39.

was 9 cubits tall.[18] Rearrangement of the poem locates the
Fall in Book IX and relates it numerically to a fairly elaborate, ironic pattern of seemingly evil persons, places and
events. The defeated angels fall nine days and nights
before they sprawl senseless on Hell's floor, there to remain nine additional days and nights before rising. The
gates of hell that spring open to evil are "thrice-three-fold"
in thickness; Eve's dream of temptation in Book IV takes
place at nine o'clock, while Adam falls (in the revised version of the poem) in Book IX at the nine-hundred and
ninety-ninth line. Such a poetic feat as this last would be
hard to credit if it stood alone. But if it does not, as I shall
show in a moment. Here, the nines are primarily interesting
because they add to a network of nines that is seemingly
Satan's, but that turns out, in reality, to be God's. All Satan's activities merely carry out the will of God. Out of evil
will come good. The nines represent defect within perfection, the perfect symbol of the Satanic state.

It would be hard to credit to Milton numerical stunts
such as having Adam fall in Book IX on the nine-hundred
and ninety-ninth line, if the instance were isolated in his
poetry. But Miss Røstvig has noted that Comus begins his
temptation speech on line six-hundred and sixty-six, the
number of the Beast of Revelation,[19] and I would add that
Milton commences his description of Death, another bes-

18. Hopper, pp. 122–23; see Rabanus, *De Universo*, XVIII, 3.
19. *The Hidden Sense*, p. 56; Miss Røstvig notes that Francesco Giorgio in his
numerological treatise *L'Harmonie du Monde* (Paris, 1579) "is most prolix" on the
subject of the number 999, "the number of the great name of God written with
letters signifying the four elements, from which he concludes that all things,
created by virtue of this great name, are limited and enclosed in their proportions
by this number."
   Replying to Miss Røstvig's study, Douglas Bush presents a caveat against over-
ingenious numerical analysis ("Calculus Racked Him," *SEL* 6 [1966]: 1–6).
Though Bush's warning is timely and important, much of its force is dissipated
by the tone of his remarks. Rather than a cogent argument against numerological
analysis, his brief article is little more than an ill-tempered outburst against
numerology's becoming "scholarly and highbrow orthodoxy." Ernest Sirluck,
SEL 6 (1966): 190–91, goes much further to demonstrate textual difficulties in
numerological readings from Milton.

tial form, at line six-hundred and sixty-six of the second book. Again, both the number of the book and the line work together in terms of a mystical significance. Two, the number of duplicity, links with the bestial number of sin and death. And this is not all. In the third book of *Paradise Lost*, Milton organizes God's discussion of Judgment so that the description of the end of evil coincides with the period that concludes on line three-hundred and thirty-three:[20]

> Then all thy Saints assembl'd, thou shalt judge
> Bad men and Angels, they arraign'd shall sink
> Beneath thy Sentence: Hell, her *numbers* full,
> *Thenceforth shall be for ever shut.*
> (III, 330–33; emphasis added)

Perhaps my readings are over-ingenious. The mathematical chances, however, against these three numerological symbols occurring by accident in *Paradise Lost* are enormous.

If we turn to a detailed consideration of the pattern in Milton's epic, certain aspects of the poem's circularity become quite noticeable almost at once. It is clear, for example, that the description of the Creation forms part of the core of the poem, reflecting on and immediately following the account of the War in Heaven. But the relationship is not simply that of contrast. Milton emphasizes the nature of the relationship by establishing a pattern of reversing action imitative of the way God, by a kind of divine peripeteia, brings good out of evil. A specific example from

20. I am indebted to one of my summer students at Mount Allison University, New Brunswick, for discovering this symbolic lineation. It is a pleasure to acknowledge William Innes's help in this and to thank him warmly for contributing so much to what was for me a most profitable and pleasant course.

Books V and VII may clarify my point and serve to introduce the ensuing analysis of the structure. Following the creation of the world the angels jubilantly sing:

>   to create
> Is greater than created to destroy.
>   (VII. 606–7)

Milton places their song in a position parallel with and opposite to Abdiel's rebuke of the rebellious crew plotting war against God:

> Then who created thee lamenting learn,
> When who can uncreate thee thou shalt know.
>   (V. 894–95)

These statements are part of the conceptual nucleus of the poem. We understand the fuller implications of that nucleus of meaning, however, when we look at the larger context in which the statements stand. Immediately following his rebuke of Satan, Abdiel returns at dawn to God and receives praise for his courage:

>   Servant of God, well done, well hast thou fought
> The better fight, who single hast maintain'd
> Against revolted multitudes the Cause
> Of Truth, *in word mightier than they in Arms.*
>   (VI. 29–32; emphasis added)

Immediately preceding the angelic song in Book VII, the Son or *Logos* returns at dawn from Creation and hears his praises sung:

>   greater now is thy return
> Than from the Giant Angels; thee that day
> Thy Thunders magnifi'd; but to create
> Is greater than created to destroy
>   (VII. 604–7)

Instead of destruction God chooses essential creation, the word rather than the sword; just so, Milton chooses to write of "higher Argument" rather than of mere martial deeds, "hitherto the only Argument/Heroic deem'd" (IX. 28–29).[21]

The twelve books of *Paradise Lost* balance in styles or genres as well as in episodes. The outer "shell" of the poem, Books I–II and XI–XII, describes the fallen worlds, first, of the rebellious angels and, last, of man himself. These are the topographical books, which survey the landscape of loss and the attempts to adapt to that landscape made by its inhabitants. These books chronicle what we would normally call heroic deeds, deeds comparable to those of the great men who filled the plains before Ilium or peopled the tales of the Old Testament. Their abundance of grandiose allusion and elaborate simile suits with their themes and overall tonality. The incomparable has been lost to the fallen; in its place they magnify their heroism by hyperbole.

Books III and X are also related stylistically. The scope of the two books is strikingly similar. Both take in all of the cosmos, from Hell's floor (if only by brief reference in Book III) to Heaven's towers. Both involve a heroic journey, Book III containing the description of Satan's bold ascent upward to the created universe and his arrival in Eden. Book X redefines this undertaking in the "aggregated soil" of that "stupendious bridge" built by Sin and Death in the wake of Satan's earlier flight. Moreover, both books generally provide a mixture of heroic, pastoral, didactic, and satiric styles. In particular, they contain most of the poem's didactic material and embody its two major satiric passages. Almost half of Book III centers on the doctrinal

---

21. In considering this illustration, it is incidentally worth noting that the natural, linear movement from left to right of center reinforces the distinction between "destroy-create." To a large extent the events of the first six books, naturally left of center, represent the sinister dominance of Satan's destructive impulses. The great creative emphases in the poem lie, for the most part, to the right of center in the divine hands.

discussion between God and the Son that sets out the justification of Godhead, or what might be called the moral
history of the poem. Book X has nothing quite so elaborate
as this protracted and heavily didactic scene, but it does
provide a briefer didactic passage in which God exonerates
the returning angelic guard from any blame for what has
transpired in Eden and once again proclaims the efficacy of
the divine scheme. This time He acts in accordance with
that scheme by sending the Son to Eden to pass the judgment that had been declared during the heavenly synod of
Book III. The two books also contain the only major satiric
passages in *Paradise Lost.* In Book III Satan touches down
on the outer shell of the created universe and affords Milton the opportunity for a delightfully derisive description
of the future Limbo of Fools, which Satan, the archetypal
fool, initiates. Here will future

> Pilgrims roam, that stray'd so far to seek
> In *Golgotha* him dead, who lives in Heav'n;
> And they who to be sure of Paradise
> Dying put on the weeds of *Dominic,*
> Or in *Franciscan* think to pass disguis'd; . . .
> Blows them transverse ten thousand Leagues awry
> Into the devious Air; then might ye see
> Cowls, Hoods and Habits with their wearers tost
> And flutter'd into Rags, then Reliques, Beads,
> Indulgences, Dispenses, Pardons, Bulls,
> The sport of Winds: all these upwhirl'd aloft
> Fly o'er the backside of the World far off
> Into a *Limbo* large and broad, since call'd
> The Paradise of Fools, to few unknown
> Long after, now unpeopl'd, and untrod.
> (III. 476–97)

From this spot Satan looks upward toward Heaven and,
"far distant" above him, sees

> Ascending by degrees magnificent
> Up to the wall of Heaven a Structure high,
> At top whereof, but far more rich appear'd

> The work as of a Kingly Palace Gate
> With Frontispiece of Diamond and Gold
> Imbellisht.
>
> (III, 502–7)

The vision of holiness closes the satiric description of the
Limbo of Fools, providing Satan with a sensual reminder
of the magnificence of wisdom and order of which he is the
antithesis.

Book X contains a comparable passage, satiric in tone.
It occurs just after the judgment of Adam and Eve in
the garden. In Hell, Sin and Death sniff with delight "the
smell/Of mortal change on Earth" (X. 272–73), and resolve to follow Satan, their "great Author," who

> thrives
> In other Worlds, and happier Seat provides
> For us his offspring dear. . . .
>
> (X. 237–39)

Like Satan in Book III, they look up toward another world,
far happier than their natural sphere and, in a discussion
that quite clearly parodies those between God and His Son,
decide to undertake the building of a great causeway between Hell and the world, following the path of Satan's
former journey. When Satan later views the finished causeway with admiration, Sin attributes it to his influence:

> O Parent, these are thy magnific deeds,
> Thy Trophies, which thou view'st as not thine own,
> Thou art thir Author and prime Architect.
>
> (X. 354–56)

Their unconscious parody continues forcefully as Satan
returns to Hell and invisibly ascends his throne. After he
observes his followers for a time from this eminence,

> At last as from a Cloud his fulgent head
> And shape Star-bright appear'd.
>
> (X. 449–50)

In imitation once again of the ways of the Godhead, he addresses his "Thrones, Dominations, Princedoms, Virtues, Powers" (X. 460) with all the pomp he wrongly associates with Heaven. But when he reports his exploits to his cohorts, parody becomes irony as the bitter mockery of God shapes his speech and produces the final, grim metamorphosis of the fallen angels into snakes, hissing their approval of Satan's activities. Their febrile response is comparable to the confused and tormented state of the future fools in Limbo, caught in a "violent cross wind" that "Blows them transverse ten thousand Leagues awry/Into the devious Air . . ." (III. 487–88).

The mixture of styles in Books III and X fulfills one criterion of epic composition. The epic was meant to embody multiple styles to match the breadth of its vision. By so doing throughout his poem, Milton follows normal Renaissance doctrine, which recognized the need for the epic to be a composite of all man's responses to the world. Girolamo Muzio noted that

> Il poema sovrano é una pittura
> De l'universo, e però in sè comprende
> Ogni stilo, ogni forma, ogni ritratto.[22]

Tasso added,

> uno sia il poema che tanta varietà di materie contegna, una la forma e la favola sua, e che tutte queste cose siano di maniera composte che l'una l'altra riguardi, l'una a l'altra corrisponda, l'una da l'altra o necessariamente o verisimilmente dependa: sì che una sola parte o tolta via o mutata di sito, il tutto ruini.[23]

22. *Rime diverse: Tre Libri di Arte Poetica, Tre Libri di Lettere in rime Sciotti, ecc.* (Venice, 1551). "The epic poem is a picture of the universe and therefore comprehends in itself all styles, all forms, all images."
23. *Discorsi dell'arte poetica. Discorso Secondo. Prose,* ed. E. Mazzali, *La letteratura italiana storia e testi* (Milan, 1959), 22: 388. "The poem that contains such great variety of matter as previously described is one; one in its form and its soul. And all these things are put together in such a manner that one relates to the other, one corresponds to the other, the one necessarily or apparently depends so much on the other that if one part is taken away or its position changed the whole is destroyed."

Books IV and IX augment the stylistic comprehensiveness of *Paradise Lost*. These are the edenic books standing opposite each other in positions that are roughly one third of the way from the beginning and end of the poem and richly treating the pastoral motif implicit throughout the poem. Book IV provides the most perfect pastoral moment. Here, as Louis Martz says,

> one may feel, more and more, how deceptive has been all that grand heroic show of human art and effort in the first two books. There will no doubt always be readers who feel as Hazlitt felt, that "Satan is the most heroic subject that ever was chosen for a poem" and that the first two books "are like two massy pillars of solid gold" . . . yet, after a reading of Book 4, their quality is subject to some question. All this show of power, Milton seems to say, is only an effort to compensate for an enormous loss.

Still, as Martz adds later, the pastoral world

> of Paradise, like all pastoral . . . cannot exist unthreatened. The beauty of the ideal, indeed, arises only within a constant pressure of corruption. Thus Satan is there.[24]

The realization of the Satanic presence is complete in Book IX, which fulfills the tragic potential inherent in Book IV as darkness engulfs the golden world of pastoral innocence. These are the two most highly dramatic books in *Paradise Lost*. They more than any others remind us of Milton's original intention to write a play called "Adam unparadiz'd" rather than an epic poem. In both books pastoral and tragedy are explicit; in each it is implicit that man will gain one at the expense of the other.

As I have indicated, Milton's opening books are heroic in style as in kind. They do not, therefore, exhibit what Milton

24. *The Paradise Within*, pp. 117 and 122. Hazlett's statements are in "Lectures on the English Poets," *Collected Works*, ed. A. R. Waller and Arnold Glover (London, 1902–04), 5:63.

came to feel were the truly epic acts. Instead, these books deal with warlike deeds "hitherto the only argument Heroic deem'd," while *his* subject offered yet "higher Argument." Books I–II recite vain endeavors of the fallen angels to respond to a world of loss, endeavors that constantly remind us of our own nature and condition. In this manner they prefigure Books XI–XII, in which Adam views man's attempts at "heroism" after the Fall. Seeking to go beyond this normal conception of the "heroic," Milton strives, I believe, to provide his audience with a loftier concept of the truly heroic response to being in the central books of the poem. The marked contrast between Books VI and VII develops from a distinction between hyperbolic rhetoric and pastoral personification. Both books are predominantly in the imperative mood, but one exhorts to death, the other to life. The "confusion of spirit and matter," which upset Dr. Johnson in contemplating the War in Heaven, is endemic to the situation Milton seeks to portray in this section of the poem. Book V begins with the pastoral mood of dawn in Eden, highlighted by the serene beauty of Adam and Eve's morning prayer: "These are thy glorious works, Parent of good" (153). This section draws to a close with Raphael's discussion of hierarchy that includes the ethereal vision of the flower:

> So from the root
> Springs lighter the green stalk, from thence the leaves
> More aery, last the bright consummate flow'r
> Spirits odorous breathes.
> (V.479–83)

From this image, so closely connected to the pastoral, the discussion abruptly changes tone, as Raphael warns Adam against disobedience and explains the reasons God has left man free to express his will. The didactic strain, itself heavier than its pastoral prelude, quickly gives way to the "high matter" of the "exploits/Of warring Spirits" (563–66). Milton marks the change in tone quite clearly as he allows his words to echo the opening of Aeneas's account to Dido of the fall of Troy (*Aeneid* II).

From the moment Satan withdraws into his northern kingdom after the elevation of the Son, his activities resemble those of the first two books of the poem. His harangue against God and the ensuing argument with Abdiel sound very much like the demonic debate in Pandemonium that we witnessed in Book II. The phony, bombastic rhetoric of general and politician fills his speeches, and he displays the typically closed mind of the reactionary:

> Natives and Sons of Heav'n possest before
> By none, and if not equal all, yet free,
> Equally free; for Orders and Degrees
> Jar not with liberty, but well consist.
> Who can in reason then or right assume
> Monarchy over such as live by right
> His equals, if in power and splendor less,
> In freedom equal? or can introduce
> Law and Edict on us, who without law
> Err not? much less for this to be our Lord,
> And look for adoration to th' abuse
> Of those Imperial Titles which assert
> Our being ordain'd to govern, not to serve?
> (V. 790–802)

To this speech Abdiel rightly replies, "O argument blasphemous, false and proud!" But when Abdiel indicts Satan on the grounds that it is folly to "dispute/With him the points of liberty, who made/Thee what thou art" (822–24), Satan haughtily rejects investigation of the subject:

> That we were form'd then say'st thou? and the work
> Of secondary hands, by task transferr'd
> From Father to his Son? strange point and new!
> Doctrine which we would know whence learnt: who saw
> When this creation was? remember'st thou

Thy making, while the Maker gave thee being?
We know no time when we were not as now;
Know none before us, self-begot, self-rais'd
By our own quick'ning power.
                              (V. 853–61)

Except for a brief interlude at the beginning of Book VI, which describes the joyous reception by God of the faithful Abdiel, the tone continues to darken, as Milton takes up the war itself. The language and imagery are heavy and hollow, Satan's speeches boastful and vain. The note struck is more often like that of Shakespeare's Achilles than of Homer's. When Satan is wounded, we see him

Gnashing for anguish and despite and shame
To find himself not matchless, and his pride
Humbl'd by such rebuke, so far beneath
His confidence to equal God in power.
                              (VI. 340–43)

Instead of his wound, Milton invites us to contemplate the bully's writhing in self-pity over the disclosure of his empty vaunts. Even Satan's mockery is self-defeating, as when he scoffs at the havoc wrought in the ranks of the loyal by his newly invented cannon, only to induce thereby his enemy's rage "against such hellish mischief fit to oppose" (636).

The point is, of course, that what seems heroic in scope proves upon investigation again and again to be absurd. The heroic postures give way to the antics of the play-ground; mountains are heaved instead of gobs of mud, but the whole affair ends too often in a mad melee in which all are involved:

They pluckt the seated Hills with all thir load,
Rocks, Waters, Woods, and by the shaggy tops
Uplifting bore them in thir hands: Amaze,
Be sure, and terror seiz'd the rebel Host,
When coming towards them so dread they saw

The bottom of the Mountains upward turn'd,
Till on those cursed Engines' triple-row
They saw them whelm'd, and all thir confidence
Under the weight of Mountains buried deep,
Themselves invaded next, and on thir heads
Main Promontories flung, which in the Air
Came shadowing, the opprest whole Legions arm'd
Thir armor help'd thir harm, crush'd in and bruis'd
Into thir substance pent, which wrought them in pain
Implacable, and many a dolorous groan.
                    (VI. 644–58)

The anticlimactic pattern of "many a dolorous groan" may stand as illustrative of the deflationary tone of most of the martial descriptions in Book VI.

Against the mock-heroic quality of Book VI, Milton sets the truly epic acts of creation. Here he immediately lightens the tone. Martial deeds fade before the joyous response of being. Vainglory gives way to the magnificent imperatives of creation, which in turn are replaced in Book VIII by the simple pastoral activities with which man re-creates himself happily in the eyes of God. What Louis Martz calls "a poetical meditation on Genesis"[25] comes to us in terms of song and dance. Martial airs are silent before the Lydian strains of the great cosmic dance of the creatures. Milton replaces the tortured images of Book VI, the inversions and hyperboles, with language that is truly "simple, sensuous, and passionate." Apart from the constant presence of the Genesis story, Milton introduces no allusions in the specific account of Creation—thereby implying its incomparableness—and stresses naturalistic detail. His eye is on the abundance of nature and its vitality, whether in describing the hand that "sow'd with Stars the Heav'n thick as a field" (375) or on the "Shoals/Of Fish that with thir Fins and shining Scales/Glide under the Green Wave" (400–2). At the close of Book VII, when Milton does introduce allusion

25. *The Paradise Within*, p. 126.

by means of a Horatian echo, he emphasizes the *beatus ille* motif from the second *Epode*:

> Thrice happy men,
> And sons of men, whom God hath thus advanc't,
> Created in his Image, there to dwell
> And worship him, and in reward to rule
> Over his Works, on Earth, in Sea, or Air,
> And multiply a Race of Worshippers
> Holy and just; thrice happy if they know
> Thir happiness, and persevere upright.
> (VII. 625–32).

The pastoral echo provides a transition from the Angelic song in praise of the Creation back to the mundane world of Eden. In the first half of Book VIII Milton completes his version of Genesis by having Adam recount for Raphael his recollection of the sixth day, when he and Eve were formed by God. As Louis Martz says, by this means Milton "deftly solves the problem of the two different Biblical accounts" of Genesis, "giving to Adam the more limited, human, anthropomorphic view of the second chapter".[26] The account allows Milton to reemphasize the simplicity of pastoral values as well, values that form the appropriate human counterpart to the epic creative activity described in Book VII. The stress remains on life values; here he defines them in terms of their humble virtues, the *vita sobria*, of a day-to-day existence amidst the bounty of nature (see figure 1).

The overall balance of styles in *Paradise Lost* complements the structural balance in the narrative events of the poem. With enough frequency to preclude coincidence, narrative events in the first half of the poem find their counterparts in the second half, repeated in inverse order.

26. Ibid., p. 127.

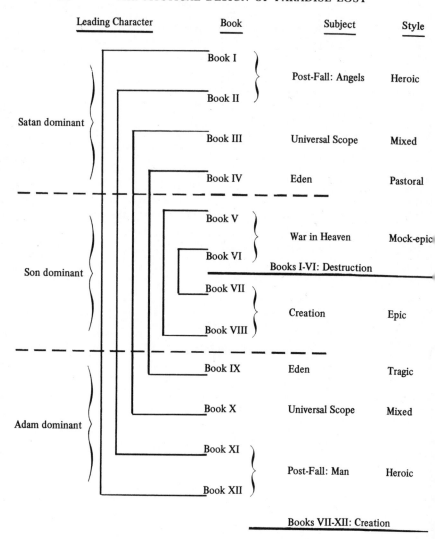

Geometric Design in PARADISE LOST

Figure 1

The pattern is the same as that described for entire books and for individual instances of the rhetorical figure *antimetabole*. Schematically, it can be indicated by the following formula: A, B, C (center of poem), B, A. In setting out the correspondences between the first and second half of the epic, I will at times of necessity be doing little more than paraphrasing the action, though I shall endeavor to be as brief as possible in this. But the main point to be kept in mind, of course, is that Milton employs narrative events to adumbrate the mystical scheme of things in very much the way that historical moments, personages, and the like, were understood to embody or shadow forth the divine plan. There was thought to be a purpose to everything if one could but perceive it. Behind apparently random events existed a pattern of accountability and, beyond faith, one of the ways traditionally given to man to discover and approximate the order of that pattern was poetry. In making his narrative antimetabolic in design, Milton imitated both the historical and the mystical pattern that locates Christ's victory over Satan at the center of man's existence. For us that victory was won by God made man, and won in the tangible world, a world of narrow, tortuous streets, a scraggy hillside, rough-hewn timbers, another's new-made tomb. The actuality of that event was brief. Yet its significance stands outside time and gains centrality in our lives by denying time and defining the inexpressible, eternal victory. Thus it is logical for Milton to place at the middle of his epic the active sign of that victory. Others have commented extensively on this point, and I shall return to some of its "temporal" aspects in the next chapter. Here I wish merely to describe the artistically logical pattern Milton created at the center of his poem and comment on how it relates the moment or point of victory to the circumference of all things. In discussing the middle of *Paradise Lost*, however, one has immediately to make a distinction between what is the expected midpoint, which comes between

Books VI and VII, and the actual, linear middle of the poem, which comes at line 766 of Book VI. Just why Milton allowed this divergence to occur is probably impossible to say with any certainty. Perhaps he thought simply of the final action leading to the end of Book VI as a unit of poetry including the midpoint. If so, his would be a concluding action, like the Virgilian description of Aeneas's descent into the underworld, the necessary action before the new world could be made manifest. Perhaps he sought merely to avoid an obvious and too easily observed consonance between statement and meaning at the midst. But speculation seems fruitless here. And the relationship between the central action and the rest of the poem further complicates the problem. In terms of the precise balancing of events on either side of the poem, Milton apparently calculates from the *end* of the central verse sentence of his epic, which comes not at line 766 of Book VI but six lines further on. More of this in a moment. First one should note that there are, in fact, a number of things happening in the central section of *Paradise Lost*. Clearly, there is continuity between the end of Book VI and the beginning of Book VII, for example, and there is even some sense of a reflexive pattern, a pattern of inversion working between Raphael's description of the end of the War in Heaven and the poet's own recognition that he must "descend from Heav'n" and return to his "Native Element," that he must begin again fashioning his work, of which "half remains unsung." Is the implication that there is more than one midpoint in man's affairs and that these affairs, like Donne's journey into Wales, shift man away from his true center, or even turn him from his salvation? Such thoughts may, in part, give rise to the complex meditation with which the poet sets out on his homeward journey. He sings more safely now of things within a "narrower bound," though he is "fall'n on evil days/On evil days though fall'n, and evil tongues." As the syntax turns at this moment, so too, one feels, Milton turns poetically and humanly to the realization that he is not alone and that his Muse is indeed his *Heavenly* Goddess, sustaining him in the darkness, guiding him surely toward his end. "Higher argument" yet remains, and the narrative of Creation begins, broadly contrasting with the account of the War in Heaven, which has preceded it.

If we return now to the midpoint in Book VI, recognizing the number of ways man may perceive the middle—in epic tradition the beginning is also a middle—we see first that the line at the exact middle of the poem is simply:

Of smoke and bickering flame, and sparkles dire.

In itself the line has no apparent significance. In its context it is the middle line of the central verse sentence of thirteen lines, which describes the ascent of the Son into his chariot and his riding forth to meet the foe. That action is what is central to the poem and to Milton's conception of the Divine scheme. "Measuring things in Heav'n by things on Earth," Milton determines for us the grand image of eternal victory by the act that immediately precipitates that victory. Poetic measurement from this center might reasonably begin, then, from line 772, concluding the description of the ascent. And there is a fair amount of internal evidence to suggest that Milton calculated from the center in just this way.

Counting forward from line 772, we note that the following twenty-eight lines complete the description of the Son's riding forth. With his Ensign blazing aloft, as he commands that "the uprooted Hills" retire "each to his place";

> they heard his voice and went
> Obsequious, Heav'n his wonted face renew'd,
> And with fresh Flow'rets Hill and Valley smil'd.
> (VI. 782–84)

Seeing His glory, the foe first grieved and then stood firm "weening to prosper . . . or to fall" (795–96). In the ensuing

twenty-three lines Milton describes how the Son takes
charge of the battle, ordering the Faithful to stand
and "from Battle rest." And in line 817, at a point forty-
five lines from the conclusion of the central action,
Milton places the Messiah's declaration of God's will:
"Therefore to mee thir doom he hath assign'd." Having
spoken thus, the Son rides forth against the enemy,
and

> his burning Wheels
> The steadfast Empyrean shook throughout,
> All but the Throne itself of God.
> (832–34)

Terrified, the enemy lose all courage, wishing that

> the Mountains now might be again
> Thrown on them as a shelter from his ire.
> (842–43)

The attack ends when the Rebels throw themselves head-
long "down from the verge of Heav'n." Their confusion
resounds through all space. Hearing

> th' unsufferable noise, Hell saw
> Heav'n ruining from Heav'n, and would have fled
> Affrighted; but strict Fate had cast too deep
> Her dark foundations, and too fast had bound.
> (867–70)

The description of the Rebels' nine-day fall through space
to Hell's floor concludes seven lines later, at a point 105
lines from the end of the central verse sentence.

Returning to the center of the epic, we see that, by counting back 105 lines from line 772, we come to line 668, the
conclusion of the description of the tumult of the second
day's battle:

> War seem'd a civil Game
> To this uproar; horrid confusion heapt
> Upon confusion rose: and now all Heav'n
> Had gone to wrack, with ruin overspread,
> (VI. 667–70)

had not God intervened. In the following thirty-line verse paragraph, Milton presents God's declaration to His Son of His will, by which he describes the victory to be won on the following morning and refers to the futility of war:

> War wearied hath perform'd what War can do,
> And to disorder'd rage let loose the reins,
> With Mountains as with Weapons arm'd, which makes
> Wild work in Heav'n, and dangerous to the main.
> (695–98)

At this point He bids His Son, "thou Mightiest in thy Father's might,/Ascend my Chariot, guide the rapid wheels/That shake Heav'n's basis" (710–12), and bring forth victory. Acknowledging His father's will—"thou in me well pleas'd, declar'st thy will" (1. 728, 45 lines from end of central verse sentence)—the Son rises "from the right hand of Glory where he sat," an action that corresponds to the dawning of the "third sacred Morn" of the struggle and the arrival of the mysterious "Chariot of Paternal Diety."

Thus, in the 211 lines at the center of *Paradise Lost,* one discovers a pronounced reflexive pattern with verbal as well as narrative parallels. The following diagram may clarify the pattern. Broadly speaking, I find that these 211 lines epitomize the overall action of *Paradise Lost,* because in the midst of apparent loss they first predict, then achieve the ultimate victory. It is a victory, however, that still remains to be won in time, the medium of man, though its eternal promise manifests itself here.

Detailed correspondences, such as those I have been discussing, do not occur throughout the central books of

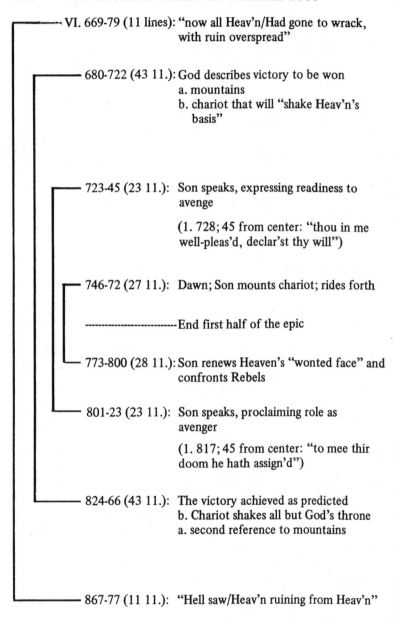

VI. 669-79 (11 lines): "now all Heav'n/Had gone to wrack, with ruin overspread"

680-722 (43 11.): God describes victory to be won
a. mountains
b. chariot that will "shake Heav'n's basis"

723-45 (23 11.): Son speaks, expressing readiness to avenge

(1. 728; 45 from center: "thou in me well-pleas'd, declar'st thy will")

746-72 (27 11.): Dawn; Son mounts chariot; rides forth

----------------------------End first half of the epic

773-800 (28 11.): Son renews Heaven's "wonted face" and confronts Rebels

801-23 (23 11.): Son speaks, proclaiming role as avenger

(1. 817; 45 from center: "to mee thir doom he hath assign'd")

824-66 (43 11.): The victory achieved as predicted
b. Chariot shakes all but God's throne
a. second reference to mountains

867-77 (11 11.): "Hell saw/Heav'n ruining from Heav'n"

Paradise Lost. Rather, Milton emphasizes, appropriately, the broad contrast between destruction and creation in the bulk of these books. Yet there are several points at which the poet reimposes the pattern, thereby strengthening the sense of a creative presence fully in control of all things. The parallel between Satan's invention of the cannon and God's proclamation of the creation provides an excellent example of this control. Occurring at points equidistant from the end of the central verse sentence of *Paradise Lost,* these passages contrast the futility of Satan's *scientia* in comparison with the *sapientia* of God.

In the aftermath of the first day's fighting, Satan encourages his downcast followers, who have experienced the "perfect misery" that is pain, by inventing the cannon (VI. 469–520). The invention is, first of all, the product of Satan's mind, but it is carried out by the "innumerable hands" of his followers as they upturn the celestial soil and see beneath "th'originals of Nature in thir crude/Conception" (509–11). As he had done earlier in describing the building of Pandemonium, here Milton emphasizes the inorganic nature of their inventive endeavors, which lead them to ransack Heaven in order to dig up veins of mineral and stone. Theirs is decidely not a *creatio ex nihilo,* nor is it conceived as such by Satan, who describes his "not uninvented that" to his followers in terms of the raw materials to be worked:

> Not uninvented that, which thou aright
> Believ'st so main to our success, I bring;
> Which of us who beholds the bright surface
> Of this Ethereous mould whereon we stand,
> This continent of spacious Heav'n, adorn'd
> With Plant, Fruit, Flow'r Ambrosial, Gems and Gold,
> Whose Eye so superficially surveys
> These things, as not to mind from whence they grow
> Deep under ground, materials dark and crude,
> Of spiritous and fiery spume, till toucht

> With Heav'n's ray, and temper'd they shoot forth
> So beauteous, op'ning to the ambient light.
> These in thir dark Nativity the Deep
> Shall yield us, pregnant with infernal flame.
>   (VI. 470–83)

The unconscious irony of "so superficially surveys" perfectly summarizes Satan's own state. For him the beauties of Heaven are superficial, bright adornments of the spacious. They are to be ignored, set aside for the crude originals of nature confined within the earth. This is the exact opposite, of course, of the Divine emblazoning on the originals of Chaos. And just as the "Engines and their Balls" that the Rebels found to bring "missive ruin" on their foes really imply their own ruin, so the subtle arts by which they concoct and adjust the sulphurous and nitrous foam serve to reduce all to "blackest grain." In seeing beyond Heaven, Satan has discovered Hell; in place of Heaven's "ambient light," he would substitute "infernal flame."

Almost exactly opposite the description of Satan's invention of the cannon, Milton places a passage of similar length (VII. 131–79) in which God declares how he "can repair/That detriment, if such it be to lose/Self-lost, and in a moment will create/Another World, out of one man a Race/Of men innumerable" (152–56). As Milton conceives of it, this creation is *ex Deo*, performed by the Word, his begotton Son. It is also a creation by withdrawal—if I may use that word without risking the hazardous waters of recent criticism.[27] His is a creation by withdrawal, however, that is in itself a stunning reversal of the demonic invention. From the boundless deep (which is Himself) God bids the world come forth. Performed by the hand of His Son,

---

27. See Robert Adam's discussion of the critical reaction to Denis Saurat's thesis (*Milton: Man and Thinker* [New York, 1925]) that Milton conceived of "creation by retraction," a notion drawn from the *Zohar* (*Ikon: John Milton and the Modern Critics* [Ithaca, N.Y., 1955], pp. 134–40.)

Creation will produce "a Race/Of men innumerable," whereas Satan's "innumerable" hoard are merely the laborers in the founding of a battery of "devilish Enginry." Satan's followers act on the deep to reduce it, thereby further restricting themselves, but God proclaims Himself "uncircumscrib'd" by his withdrawal. And whereas Satan's invention will turn "spacious Heav'n" momentarily into a hellish battlefield, God's munificence foresees that men "by degrees of merit rais'd" will "open to themselves at length the way/Up hither . . ./And Earth be chang'd to Heav'n, and Heav'n to Earth,/One Kingdom, Joy and Union without end" (VII. 157–61).

The actual account of Creation (VII. 192–581) contrasts with the extended description of the first day and night of the War in Heaven (VI. 56–467). Though it is of some interest to note that these passages are comparable in length, there is little that is parallel in them, as I have said. But the description of Creation concludes with the triumphant return of the Son to Heaven and the jubilant song of the angels: "to create/Is greater than created to destroy" (VII. 581–632—a passage that begins 721 lines from the end of the central verse sentence of the epic), while the account of the war is immediately preceded by the return of Abdiel, who singly "maintain'd/Against revolted multitudes the Cause/Of Truth." Like the Son after him, he is greeted by "acclamations loud," having "fought/The better fight . . . in word mightier than they in Arms" (VI. 1–55 —ending 718 lines from central sentence). Milton thus clearly marks off the major contrast between destruction and creation by encircling it with parallel passages emphasizing the creative principle of the Word.

If we work back still further away from the center, we find that the parallels between Books V and VIII are at least as numerous and significant to the overall sense of the mystical in the epic as those we have been studying. The main relationships about which I wish to speak begin in Book V with the dispatch of Raphael on his mission to warn Adam and Eve of the impending danger from Satan. The relationships, likewise, conclude with Raphael, this time as he departs from Eden back toward Heaven, having carried out his charge. The first event takes place at dawn in Heaven, the second at dusk in Eden. Both occur at precisely the same spot in relation to the center of the epic. Raphael departs from Heaven at a point 1,433 lines from the end of the central verse sentence. He leaves Eden to return to Heaven at a point that is also 1,433 lines from the center. Like several other examples that I have cited earlier, this numerical consonance seems hard to credit to chance. Unless we are inclined to stand like Rosencrantz and Guildenstern desperately flipping coins on an indifferent morning, we ought probably to accept this consonance as a further manifestation of Milton's mathematical bent and of his poem's mystical meaning.

At any rate, with these two moments defined, Milton proceeds to develop a complex series of parallels between Books V and VIII. In seeking out these relationships, however, one is in constant danger of ending "in wand'ring mazes lost." It has seemed wise, therefore, to subdivide these books in what is hopefully not too arbitrary a fashion and thereby provide a thread by which we can trace our way back through the, at times, labyrinthine design. I here distinguish four main sections of Book V, from Raphael's departure for Eden to the description of Abdiel's flight from the councils of the rebel angels with which Milton closes the book, and set them against four comparable passages in Book VIII:

A   Book V. 246–391: 155 lines (1433–1289 from end of central section: VI. 772)

B   " "   391–576: 185 lines (1289–1104 from VI. 772)

C   " "   577–693: 116 lines (1103–987 from VI. 772)

D	" "	694–907:	213 lines (986–773 from VI. 772)
D_1	Book VIII.	1-216:	216 lines (781-996 from VI. 772)
C_1	" "	216–356:	140 lines (997- 1136 from VI. 772)
B_1	" "	357–490:	133 lines (1137–1269 from VI. 772)
A_1	" "	491–653:	162 lines (1270–1433 from VI. 772)

Let me begin with a comparison of the A sections of these books. Immediately following the dispatch of Raphael by God, Milton sets out a forty-four line description of his flight through the created universe and of his angelic shape, which he reassumes on his arrival at the "eastern cliff of Paradise." The passage is rapid and colorful; its emphasis is on the nature of Raphael's appearance and flight. As such it is one of several passages in *Paradise Lost* in which Milton introduces a touch of angelic lore of the kind that would have delighted a seventeenth-century reader less for its quaintness than for its informative aspects. The treatment of Raphael's flight and appearance has its parallel in the forty-two line passage of Book VIII just prior to his departure from Eden. Here in response to a question by Adam, Raphael, glowing "celestial rosy red" describes how the heavenly spirits actively express their love one for another. The imminent setting of the sun, however, provides him with an excuse to curtail the discussion of a perhaps too intimate subject.

In Book V Adam sees Raphael approach, calls to Eve to behold the splendid sight, and then gently dispatches her to prepare for their guest. She, "on hospitable thoughts intent," bounteously gathers food and "strews the ground/ With rose and odours from the shrub unfum'd." Meanwhile Adam goes out to meet Raphael,

> though not aw'd,
> Yet with submiss approach and reverence meek,
> As to a superior Nature, bowing low.
> (358–60).

As Adam and Raphael arrive at the bower, Milton defines
Eve in terms of her essential fruitfulness:

> So to the Silvan Lodge
> They came, that like *Pomona's* Arbor smil'd
> With flow'rets deck't and fragrant smells; but *Eve*
> Undeck't, save with herself more lovely fair
> Than Wood-Nymph, or the fairest Goddess feign'd
> Of three that in Mount *Ida* naked strove,
> Stood to entertain her guest from Heav'n; no veil
> Shee needed, Virtue-proof, no thought infirm
> Alter'd her cheek.
>   (V. 377–85).

Though a discordant note lies beneath the surface of these
lines by virtue of the allusion which compares Eve to
Venus, to whom Paris awarded the Apple of Discord, the
primary emphasis is on Eve's innocent beauty and on her
hospitality amid the bounty of nature. Raphael's greeting
carries the motif forward and provides Milton with an opportunity markedly to compare Eve with Mary. On Eve

> the Angel *Hail*
> Bestow'd, the holy salutation us'd
> Long after to blest *Mary*, second *Eve*.
>   Hail Mother of Mankind, whose fruitful Womb
> Shall fill the World more numerous with thy Sons
> Than with these various fruits the Trees of God
> Have heap'd this Table.
>   (V.385–91)

Eve's role as the mother of mankind tallies with her bounty
as hostess, and the identification with Mary links her as
much with man's salvation as with his damnation. The An-

gelic "Hail" makes the specific connection; it is the *Ave* that implies the future reversal of the wrong done to man through *Eva*.

The implications of that link are further manifested when we compare these lines with their counterpart in Book VIII. As the related passage in Book V ended with Raphael's greeting of Eve, linking her name with Mary's, so the one in Book VIII begins with Adam's naming and defining the essential nature of his newly created helpmate:

> I now see
> Bone of my Bone, Flesh of my Flesh, my Self
> Before me; Woman is her Name, of Man
> Extracted; for this cause he shall forego
> Father and Mother, and to his Wife adhere;
> And they shall be one Flesh, one Heart, one Soul.
> (VIII. 494–99)

In thanking God for this most precious gift, Adam has innocently, unintentionally, but no less prophetically, defined Eve for us and given us an insight into his own crucial weakness. As man he will forgo his Father for Eve. The Creator will be supplanted by the creature. In characterizing Eve as Woman, moreover, Adam stresses less the general fecundity of her nature as "mother of mankind" than the singleness of her beauty and femininity as they affect him. The tone is almost entirely sensual, despite the elaborate praise of her "virgin-modesty,/Her virtue and the conscience of her worth," lines that provide a dim echo of her unveiled yet "virtue-proof" demeanor before Raphael (V. 376–77). Having named her, Adam leads Eve to their nuptial bower, while

> all Heav'n,
> And happy Constellations on that hour
> Shed thir selectest influence; the Earth
> Gave sign of gratulation, and each Hill;

> Joyous of Birds; fresh Gales and gentle Airs
> Whisper'd it to the Woods, and from thir wings
> Flung Rose, flung Odors from the spicy Shrub,
> Disporting, till the amorous Bird of Night
> Sung Spousal, and bid haste the Ev'ning Star
> On his Hill top, to light the bridal Lamp.
>   (VIII. 511–20)

Here it is nature and not Eve creating the proper atmosphere, but the parallel is unmistakable: for Raphael's visit, Eve "strews the ground/With Rose and Odors from the shrub unfum'd" (V. 348–49). In addition to the repetition of rose, odor and shrub, Milton's use of "spicy" parallels his earlier description of the shrub as "unfum'd," that is, unburned, in reference to the natural perfume given off by the bush. The allusion to Venus, the evening star, in the latter passage, may also be intended to provide an echo of the earlier description of Eve bringing food to Adam and Raphael. As she waits on them "no thought infirm" altered her cheek; on their wedding night Adam leads her "blushing like the Morn" to their nuptial bower. Milton clearly intends nothing inappropriate in speaking of Adam and Eve's first night together. It is all as natural as the meal with Raphael. But the mood has changed slightly from Eve's "hospitable thoughts" and Adam's "reverence meek" toward Raphael as "to a superior Nature, bowing low," to the feelings of "commotion strange" experienced by Adam as he leads Eve to their bower, and his self-abasement, though he well understands her "in the prime end/Of Nature . . . th'inferior." Indeed, as Adam describes Eve to Raphael and recounts their first moments together, he gradually rises to that high-flown praise of her beauty and its power over him which leads Raphael gently to rebuke him: "be not diffident/Of Wisdom . . . In Loving thou dost well, in passion not" (562–88).

The second section of Book V, opening with a brief glance at the idyllic repast, largely consists of an elaborate definition of the hierarchical principle of the universe. Acknowledging that "one Celestial Father gives to all," Adam humbly but hesitantly offers food to his angelic guest. Raphael reassures him, noting that

> food alike those pure
> Intelligential substances require
> As doth your Rational;
> (V. 407–9)

indeed, sustenance is a universal need, worked out through the principle that in all things the "grosser feeds the purer." Raphael will go on at Adam's prompting to a more elaborate description of the hierarchical pattern of the world, but Milton interrupts the forward progress of his narrative to praise the naked beauty and innocence of Eve as she "at Table . . . Minister'd." Hers is an "innocence/ Deserving Paradise," perfectly in accord with the order of things. Continuing his discussion of the angelic nature, Raphael illustrates the overriding structure of the universe by means of the example of the flower, in which

> from the root
> Springs lighter the green stalk, from thence the leaves
> More aery, last the bright consummate flow'r
> Spirits ordorous breathes.
> (V. 479–82)

He adds that man and angel differ "but in degree" and that, if "man be found obedient," he will at last turn "all to spirit," joining the angelic ranks in Heaven. Adam asks what Raphael implies by the conditional mention of obedience, and is told:

> That thou art happy, owe to God;
> That thou continu'st such, owe to thyself.
> (520–21)

Prompted still further by Adam, Raphael begins his account of past events in Heaven, indicating that he will delineate these occurrences "by lik'ning spiritual to corporal forms."

The comparable section of Book VIII ends (as the section in Book V began) with a discussion of hierarchy and a picture of Eve as she is created and brought to Adam by God. She is a creature, as Adam says,

> Manlike, but different sex, so lovely fair,
> That what seem'd fair in all the World, seem'd now
> Mean, or in her summ'd up, in her contain'd
> And in her looks, which from that time infus'd
> Sweetness in my heart, unfelt before,
> And into all things from her Air inspir'd
> The spirit of love and amorous delight.
> (VIII. 471–77)

This is that "innocence/Deserving Paradise" which Milton proclaimed in Book V, an innocence and beauty that, as he said, might have given

> the Sons of God excuse to have been
> Enamour'd at that sight; but in those hearts
> Love unlibidinous reign'd; not jealousy
> Was understood, the injur'd Lover's Hell.
> (V. 447–50)

She is the Maker's supreme gift, but Adam has argued for her creation. In the passage following the naming of the beasts and preceding Eve's actual creation, Milton dramatizes this argument. Recognizing that God surpasses far his naming, Adam asks

> how may I
> Adore thee, Author of this Universe,
> And all this good to man, for whose well being

> So amply, and with hands so liberal
> . . . hast provided all things . . .?
> (VIII. 359–63)

And he goes on to observe that with him he sees "not who partakes." God argues both the abundance of His creation and the example of His own solitariness to lessen Adam's feelings of isolation. But Adam protests that God is Himself perfect. "Not so is Man,/But in degree," prompting "his desire/By conversation with his like to help,/Or solace his defects" (VIII. 416–19). Initially God had smiled benignly at Adam's request, saying:

> A nice and subtle happiness I see
> Thou to thyself proposest, in the choice
> Of thy Associates, *Adam,* and wilt taste
> No pleasure, though in pleasure, solitary.
> (399–402)

Yet he finally consents, admitting that "Thus far to try thee, *Adam,* was I pleas'd" . . . (437).

Notions of degree, the sense of Eve's beauty and its power, the relationship of happiness to self as providing an essential aspect of universal sustenance—these are the basic motifs emphasized here and in the comparable section of Book V. The essence of Adam's request is acceptable to God, but its implications lead to a larger question of the integrity of the self, a question suggested by the naming of Eve, "Woman . . . of Man/Extracted." She is man's helpmate; by her and through her man can know perfect union. But as she is a part of man, that union will of necessity be a reunion of the divided self.

The third, or "C" section, of Book V (lines 578–693) enriches the pattern already established. Following Raphael's acknowledgment that he must liken "spiritual to corporal" forms to make his relation intelligible to Adam, the angel recounts the events surrounding the Elevation of the

Son. That "day" begins with the gathering of the "empyreal Host/Of Angels by Imperial summons call'd" (V. 583–84). Encircling God, who speaks "as from a flaming Mount, whose top/Brightness had made invisible," the angels hear Him appoint His Son their Head. They are to abide under his "great Vice-gerent Reign . . . United as one individual Soul/For ever happy" (598–611). But God warns against disobedience, pronouncing the interdiction: "him who disobeys/Mee disobeys." Such an act will constitute a breaking of union and will result in the casting out into "utter darkness" of the fallen. At this pronouncement, Milton says, "all seem'd well pleas'd, all seem'd, but were not all." As evening approaches, tables are set and a banquet redolent of God's bounty suddenly appears (V. 631–41). Following the feast "grateful Twilight . . . and roseate Dews" dispose "All but the unsleeping eyes of God to rest" (645–47). It is at this moment that Satan—"so call him now," says Raphael, "his former name/Is heard no more in Heav'n"—steals away at midnight to his northern kingdom to prepare "fit entertainment to receive our King/The Great *Messiah*" (690–91).

With Satan's sarcasm fresh in our minds, let us turn to the beginning of the "C" section of Book VIII. Here Raphael tells Adam of his "voyage uncouth and obscure" to the gates of Hell, where he and his legion were to keep watch to see that "none thence issu'd forth a spy" while the Son created man. Raphael goes on to say

> Fast we found, fast shut
> The dismal Gates, and barricado'd strong;
> But long ere our approaching heard within
> Noise, other than the sound of Dance or Song,
> Torment, and loud lament, and furious rage.
> (VIII. 240–44)

Across the gulf come the echoes, and we realize that it is Satan and his crew who have "fit entertainment" found. As they have denied the dance and song of Heaven, so they have affirmed their eternal torment and furious rage.

Raphael and his legion return to Heaven, "up to the coasts of Light/Ere Sabbath Ev'ning." Thus it is that Raphael is ignorant of the details of Adam's creation and is ready to learn of that event from his host. The essence of Adam's account, as it reflects Book V, is his awakening to the profuseness, the bounty of God, who appears before Adam like a dream to raise him up by the hand and lead him to Eden, where He pronounces the divine interdiction:

> of the Tree whose operation brings
> Knowledge of good or ill, which I have set
> The Pledge of thy Obedience and thy Faith,
> Amid the Garden by the Tree of Life,
> Remember what I warn thee, shun to taste,
> And shun the bitter consequence: for know,
> The day thou eat'st thereof, my sole command
> Transgrest, inevitably thou shalt die;
> From that day mortal, and this happy State
> Shalt lose, expell'd from hence into a World
> Of woe and sorrow.
>
> (VIII. 323–33)

The section ends when God summons the beasts to Adam to receive their names and "pay [him] fealty/With low subjection," as in Book V the Angels had been summoned by God to hear pronounced the name of the Son and to do Him fit homage.

The closing portion of Book V ends with Abdiel's withdrawal from the councils of evil to return to the divine presence, while the action at the beginning of Book VIII includes the moment of Eve's withdrawal from the company of Adam and Raphael, as they turn to "studious thoughts abstruse." She returns to the fruits and flowers of her "nursery", which "at her coming sprung/And toucht by her fair tendance gladlier grew." The "abstruse thoughts" that the others pursue center on Adam's inquiry "concerning celestial Motions" and Raphael's doubtful

reply that defines celestial speculation in relation to the
proper study of mankind. At the exact center of Raphael's
reply, we recall, Raphael asks, "What if the Sun/Be Centre
to the World?" and goes on to stress that all debate is fuitle
and of minor import against a knowledge of the true presence at the center of all things of the eternal goodness of
the Godhead. The passage has its parallel in the lengthy
debate between Satan and Abdiel about the true nature of
the divinity. In the course of that debate, Satan first apes
the creator in speech and demeanor, addressing his followers from on high "in imitation of that Mount whereon/
Messiah was declar'd in sight of Heav'n" (764–65), and ends
by denying, indeed, that he was ever created at all:

> That we were form'd then say'st thou? and the work
> Of secondary hands, by task transferr'd
> From Father to his Son? strange point and new!
> Doctrine which we would know whence learnt: who saw
> When this creation was? remember'st thou
> Thy making, while the Maker gave thee being?
> (V. 853–58)

Though in words similar to Adam's admission to Raphael
in Book VIII that "for Man to tell how human Life began/Is
hard; for who himself beginning knew?" (250–51), Adam's
recognition leads at once into an imaginative attempt to
evoke that moment as fully as possible. The overall debate
between Abdiel and Satan, however, is almost a paradigm
for the futile disputes and "quaint Opinions wide" that
Raphael speaks of in relation to man's attempts to know the
true nature of the universe. It is also perhaps worth noting
that in the midst of the discussion between Satan and Abdiel, the latter disdainfully remarks:

> But to grant it thee unjust,
> That equal over equals Monarch Reign:
> *Thyself though great and glorious dost thou count,*

> Or all Angelic Nature join'd in one,
> Equal to him begotten Son, by whom
> As by his Word the mighty Father made
> All things, ev'n thee.
>
> (831–37; emphasis added)

At the exact center of their debate, that is, Abdiel points out the fallacious centrality that Satan would assume in relation to the truth of Godhead. To study centralities, celestial or otherwise is, ultimately, to engage in futile or self-serving endeavor unless the concept of the absolute center that is God informs all. Raphael's query ends not in a denial of investigation or a contradiction of appearances, but in an affirmation urging the need to "be lowly wise." Man must think only what concerns him and live like Adam, "contented that thus far hath been reveal'd/Not of Earth only but of highest Heav'n" (VIII. 173–78). Though Raphael enjoins Adam to be "lowly wise," however, it is clear that Adam's intellectual curiosity manifests his positive, outgoing personality. In this he is the antithesis of Satan, whose denial of the Creator at the close of Book V marks the nihilism at the very core of his being. Thus in a sense Book V ends where Book VIII begins, in the midst of "thoughts abstruse." But thought for Satan leads only to denial—of his maker, first, and finally of himself; for Adam it strengthens him in humility, making the world he would know more fully open to him.

At this point a discussion of the similarities between Books IV and IX would seem to follow. But these books do not maintain the reversing pattern. It is not until Raphael's arrival in Eden as God's emissary that the emphasis shifts and we feel an overlay of the mysteriously celestial. The few hours of Raphael's presence in Eden are deliciously protracted; time seems hardly to be a factor when we learn in

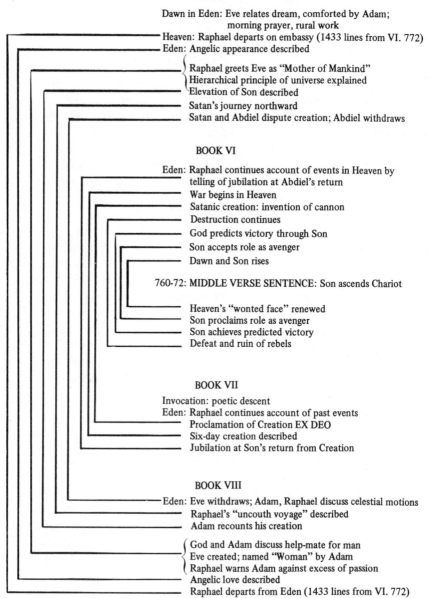

Selected parallels from central books of PARADISE LOST

Figure 2

Book VIII, line 210, for example, that Adam and Raphael remain seated on the grass, enjoying the meal prepared by Eve, lingering over their repast, unhurried, speaking almost casually, at times, of the infinite. Before Raphael's arrival, however, Milton provides us with a set of rather rapidly paced actions. Adam and Eve awake, discuss her disturbing dream of the night before, fall to prayer, and then hasten to their "morning's rural work." God beholds them with interest and concern, and dispatches Raphael, who brings with him a suggestion of the still timelessness at the center of eternity.

In Books IV and IX, however, the sequential emphasis exists by itself. Events repeat themselves in the same order, and we watch the tragic events of Book IX unfold, experiencing the sadness and nostalgia of *déjà vu*. Somehow we have seen this all before; we know what will happen next, but it is not quite right! Things have changed, and with the Fall Satan seems momentarily, at least, to have imposed his will on the organic design of God's universe. But his impact is only momentary in terms of the total vision of the poem, and we soon return to the predominant structural pattern. Since these two books are so evidently different from the others, I would like to bypass them now, examining in the next chapter how their chronological force operates in relation to the temporal structure of the poem.

Putting Books IV and IX aside for the moment, then, we may look at the structural relationships evident in Books III and X. As I have said, these books are similar in the vastness of their scope and the variety of their styles. They also continue the reversing pattern of the poem, lending physical emphasis to the process of good supplanting evil. Both books divide into three parallel sections. The first section of Book III begins with Milton's hymn to "holy Light" and then describes the dialogue in Heaven between God and the Son, during which God defines his plan ultimately to defeat forever the forces of evil. In response to his program, the multitude of Angels fill Heaven with "loud Hosannas" to the "Author of all being,/Fountain of Light," casting their heavenly crowns "inwove with Amarant" to the ground, an action which, incidentally, provides Milton with an opportunity to describe that "flow'r which once/in paradise, fast by the Tree of Life/Began to bloom." This section (III. 1–415) is followed by a briefer section (416–554) describing Satan's landing on the "firm opacous Globe" of the newly created universe, which

> now seems a boundless Continent
> Dark, waste, and wild, under the frown of Night
> Starless expos'd, and ever-threat'ning storms
> Of *Chaos* blust'ring round, inclement sky.
> (III. 423–26)

By landing there, as I have said, Satan defines the place as the future Limbo of Fools through his presence as the first of time's fools. The third section of Book III begins with the description of Satan's flight through "the World's first region" toward the earth. In this passage Milton depicts Satan standing in the Sun, the sky's "great Luminary/Aloof" and characterizes the beneficent force of the "all-cheering Lamp" operating througout the universe. As Martin Price has pointed out,

> Milton presents the sun as the visible symbol of God in his
> ordered universe, both transcendent and immanent. . . . The
> light is mysterious and remote, but it becomes in turn the
> ordering principle of time and the source of life. . . . Finally,
> it is associated with the warmth that penetrates, like grace,
> unseen and breeds precious gems within the earth or godlike
> powers within man.[28]

The final events of this section and book present Satan's conversation with Uriel and his landing on Mt. Niphates.

28. *To the Palace of Wisdom* (New York, 1964), pp. 8–9.

Though much longer, Book X parallels Book III in its organization. Beginning with a reference to the evil done in Paradise by Satan, Book X describes the angelic guard returning to Heaven, there to be absolved of blame for allowing Satan access to man. God and the Son speak briefly of the implications of the Fall. The primary concern of this brief section is to confirm once again the justice and mercy of God's intentions. In this sense the passage beginning on line 55, in which God asks "whom shall I send to judge them?", couched in terms of the radiant light of God's grace as it operates through the Son, may parallel the description in Book III of the cosmic influence of the sun. It is followed by a dramatically brief reference to the Son's flight from Heaven to Eden (11. 85–91). Compared with the stupendous endeavor of Satan's flight in Book III, the Son's descent is brief and easy, perhaps emblematic of the simplicity of all God's efforts. In Eden the Son passes judgment on Adam, Eve, the Serpent, and Satan, but ends by clothing the saddenend couple, thus not disdaining "to begin/Thenceforth the form of servant to assume." The Son's ministry contrasts sharply with the malignity of Satan, seized with envy at the sight of the beauty of the world (III. 540–54).

The middle section of Book X (lines 229–613) describes the aftermath of the Fall as it affects Satan, Sin, and Death. The section is much longer than its counterpart in Book III, the Limbo of Fools passage, but the scope is surely appropriate as an implicit commentary of the repercussions of Satan's acts. The passages are parallel in satiric tone. There is parody in Book X of the Heavenly scene that Book III put before us. The force of the parallels is particularly strong as Satan returns to Hell and describes for his followers how he tempted man with an apple, and how God "thereat-/Offended, worth your laughter, hath giv'n up/Both his beloved man and all his World" . . . (487–89). Expecting applause, Satan receives a "dismal universal hiss," the appropriate counterpart, from the moral point of view of the poem, to the angelic Hosannas of Book III. The devils, metamorphosed into serpents, swarm out of Pandemonium and encounter

> A Grove hard by, sprung up with this thir change,
> His will who reigns above, to aggravate
> Thir penance, laden with fair Fruit, like that
> Which grew in Paradise.
>
> (X. 548–51)

Paralleling the description of that heavenly plant, Amaranth, that once had grown in Paradise and now flourishes only in Heaven, Milton rewards the denizens of Hell with a tempting grove of trees like that which grew in Paradise, but a grove whose fruit is only bitter ashes. The serpents' metamorphosis and the following description, of God's bidding "his Angels turn askance/The Poles of Earth" (X. 668–69) to "affect the Earth with cold and heat/Scarce tolerable" (X. 653–54), provides a lengthy counterpart to the briefer passage in Book III in which Milton describes the "ever-threat'ning storms/Of *Chaos* blust'ring round" and "inclement" skies as Satan lands on the shell of the universe.

Book X closes with the agonizing drama of the soul in which Adam and Eve confront their loss and determine ultimately to work through the curse against Satan and seek God's forgiveness in prayer. In the course of their discussion, Adam offers to take upon himself all the blame for their sins (X. 952–65). After considering and discarding several possible courses of action, they decide to persevere and seek God's grace, recognizing how labor will sustain them and "how much more" may be gained from God, who has clothed them, through prayer, which may open his ear

> and his heart to pity incline,
> And teach us further by what means to shun

Th' inclement Seasons, Rain, Ice, Hail and Snow,
Which now the Sky with various Face begins
To show us in this Mountain.
                              (X. 1061–65)

With this recognition they fall to prayers of supplication, emitting sighs and tears "of sorrow unfeign'd, and humiliation meek." This whole section is comparable in a number of ways to the opening section of Book III. The dialogue between Adam and Eve balances with that between God and the Son in III. Adam's desire to take upon him all blame for the Fall echoes God's specific determination of the role of his Son as Savior:

> Be thou in *Adam's* room
> The Head of all mankind, though *Adam's* Son
> As in him perish all men, so in thee
> As from a second root shall be restor'd,
> As many as are restor'd, without thee none.
>   (III. 285–89)

As Book X ends with reference to the seasons and the mitigating effect of prayer, so III has begun with Milton's great hymn to heavenly light, in which he petitions that God's light shine within him to "irradiate" his darkness, bringing inner light to the blind poet for whom the "sight of vernal bloom" with the returning seasons will never again be possible in this world (see fig. 3).

The old ten-book format inseparably links the structural relationships of Books II and XI with a discussion of I and XII, strongly indicating, as I have said, that the "geometric" design of *Paradise Lost* antedates any division of the poem into books. Book II opens with Satan high enthroned in Pandemonium speaking to his cohorts preliminary to the grand consultation. His speech concerns his place as chief of the fallen angels and stresses the complete absence of envy in Hell:

BOOK III

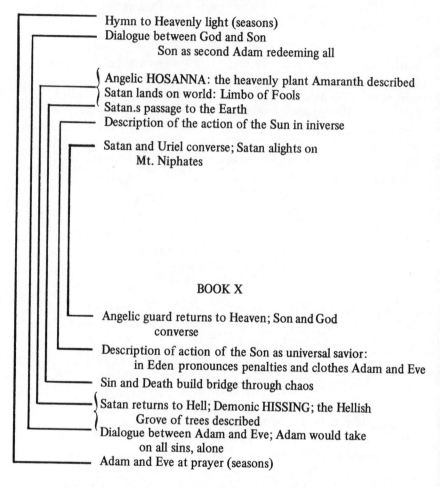

Hymn to Heavenly light (seasons)
Dialogue between God and Son
    Son as second Adam redeeming all

Angelic HOSANNA: the heavenly plant Amaranth described
Satan lands on world: Limbo of Fools
Satan.s passage to the Earth
Description of the action of the Sun in iniverse

Satan and Uriel converse; Satan alights on
    Mt. Niphates

BOOK X

Angelic guard returns to Heaven; Son and God
    converse

Description of action of the Son as universal savior:
    in Eden pronounces penalties and clothes Adam and Eve

Sin and Death build bridge through chaos

Satan returns to Hell; Demonic HISSING; the Hellish
    Grove of trees described
Dialogue between Adam and Eve; Adam would take
    on all sins, alone

Adam and Eve at prayer (seasons)

Selected Parallels from Books III and X of PARADISE LOST

Figure 3

> who here
> Will envy whom the highest place exposes
> Foremost to stand against the Thunderer's aim
> Your bulwark, and condemns to greatest share
> Of endless pain?
>
> (II. 26–30)

The speech is an ironic disclaimer, as we see later when Satan acts quickly to avoid sharing the dangers and glory of his proposed expedition to the new world with any of his followers (II. 465–66). It also thinly cloaks his wrath and determination to persist in evil. He seeks encouragement by reasoning

> From this descent
> Celestial Virtues rising, will appear
> More glorious and more dread than from no fall,
> And trust themselves to fear no second fate,
>
> (II. 14–17)

and affirms that lack of envy will provide the advantage of "union, and firm faith" by which

> we now return
> To claim our just inheritance of old.
>
> (37–38)

The whole speech has its counterpart at the close of Book XI, when Michael reveals to Adam the results of the Flood. Michael tells him that after the Flood God "relents" and—unlike Satan—"willingly remits his Ire" (XI. 885) against man by establishing through the rainbow his covenant never again to destroy man or his world by water. Both sections concern a program of "revenge" on man. God's has been openly realized in the Flood and in His treating with Noah to preserve what is best among His creatures. Satan's speech provides a prelude to the debate that he secretly directs through Beelzebub. Beelzebub verbalizes the program of revenge, but it has been Satan all along who has had the plan in mind. The difference in maneuvering is typical of the difference between the open, though seemingly autocratic rule of God and the underhanded activities of Satan, devious and tyrannical even in relation to his own followers. To implement his preconceived program Satan has called a grand consultation and allows an apparently open parliamanetary debate to ensue. But Beelzebub waits for the propitious moment to introduce the real matter of the debate:

> There is a place
> (If ancient and prophetic fame in Heav'n
> Err not) another World, the happy seat
> Of some new Race call'd *Man,* about this time
> To be created like to us, though less
> In power and excellence, but favor'd more
> Of him who rules above; so was his will
> Pronounc'd among the Gods, and by an Oath,
> That shook Heav'n's whole circumference, confirm'd.
> Thither let us bend all our thoughts, to learn
> What creatures there inhabit, of what mould,
> Or substance, how endu'd, and what thir Power,
> And where thir weakness, how attempted best,
> By force or subtlety: . . .
> Seduce them to our Party, that thir God
> May prove thir foe, and with repenting hand
> Abolish his own works.
>
> (II. 345–58, 368–70)

The machinations of Satan and Beelzebub at this point may intrigue us, but we should not be taken in by them. God's activities in Book XI emphasize their falsity. Upon hearing the prayers of Adam and Eve and receiving the supplication of the Son in their favor, God calls a synod (67ff.) at which he directly proposes his plan for man—which He, too, has had in mind "from the beginning," though that phrase, of course, has no relevance to God.

Returning to the reversing pattern in the two books, we recognize that Moloch's speech in favor of "open war" (II.

51–105) parallels Enoch's protests against "sword law," which conclude the "council in the City Gates," and Adam's first vision of the phenomenon of war (XI. 638–673). Belial speaks after Moloch, fair Belial who

> seem'd
> For dignity compos'd and high exploit:
> But all was false and hollow.
>   (II. 110–12)

He counsels "ignoble ease, and peaceful sloth" (II. 227). His long speech contrasts with the discussion in Book XI between Adam and Michael of the "Tents of Wickedness" and

> that fair female Troop . . . that seem'd
> Of Goddesses, so blithe, so smooth, so gay,
> Yet empty of all good.
>   (XI. 614–16)

At first, this vision of the original "marriage rites" (XI. 591) had appeared to Adam

> Much better . . . and more hope
> Of peaceful days portends, than those two past;
> Those were of hate and death.
>   (XI. 599–601)

Belial's counsel in Book II had similarly been based on the mistaken premise that if the Fallen angels merely "sustain and bear" their doom,

> Our Supreme Foe in time may much remit
> His Anger, and perhaps thus far remov'd
> Not mind us not offending, . . .
>   whence these raging fires
> Will slack'n.
>   (II. 210–14)

Michael's reply to Adam in Book XI provides an appropriate comment on both misconceptions of the future:

> Judge not what is best
> By pleasure, though to Nature seeming meet.
> (XI. 603–4)

In the grand consultation of Book II, Mammon follows Belial with a proposal to make a Heaven out of Hell, only to be countered by Beelzebub, who offers the plan of revenge on God through man. While I find no precise counterparts in Book XI to the speeches of Mammon and Beelzebub, there is a conceptual link, perhaps, between Mammon's absurd proposal to make Heaven in Hell and Michael's warning to Adam of the need to be temperate:

> Nor love thy Life, nor hate; but what thou liv'st
> Live well.
> (XI. 553–55)

Throughout the debate in Hell the fallen angels confuse the essence of time and place. Belial thinks that God may "in time" remit his ire, but Belial fails to understand, of course, that time is essentially their element, not God's. The same order of miscalculation is present in his belief that God is "far remov'd" and may not mind therefore "us not offending." But it is they who are far removed. Space is for them, as Jackson Cope says, the "ambient of pain".[29] Thus, when Mammon suggests that the Devils create Heaven in Hell, he confuses essence with place and would substitute the external for the internal value.

The vision in Book XI of Abel's murder at the hands of Cain, and the long, grim catalogue of the shapes Death will

29. *The Metaphoric Structure of* Paradise Lost, p. 58.

take in coming to man, may remind us of Beelzebub's plan, which will result in man's death. A more precise set of correspondences emerges, however, between Adam's vision of death and the confrontation in Book II between Satan and the hideous shape of Death at Hell's gates. Adam's anguish after witnessing the murder of Abel,

> have I now seen Death? . . . O sight
> Of terror, foul and ugly to behold,
>   (XI. 462–65)

is similar to Satan's reaction to the revelation by Sin that he faces his own son in the grotesque monster Death:

> I know thee not, not ever saw till now
> Sight more detestable than him and thee.
>   (II. 744–45)

In both passages Death threatens. In Book XI he hovers above the sick and dying in the vision of the lazar-house:

> And over them triumphant Death his Dart
> Shook, but delay'd to strike,
>   (XI. 491–92)

while in Book II, Death threatens Satan:

> black it stood as Night,
> Fierce as ten Furies, terrible as Hell,
> And shook a dreadful Dart.
>   (II. 670–72)

Other parallels between the two books may be summarized briefly. In Book II, as a result of the debate in Hell, Satan offers himself as a scout to reconnoiter for his forces. A blast of Doric trumpets proclaims his valor and closes the deliberations (II. 514–20). While Satan flies toward the gates of Hell, those left behind undertake various activities to while away the time until their leader's return. The more adventurous set out

> to discover wide
> That dismal World,
>
> (II. 571–72)

and,

> roving on
> In confus'd march forlorn, th' advent'rous Bands
> With shudd'ring horror pale, and eyes aghast
> View'd first thir lamentable lot, and found
> No rest: through many a dark and dreary Vale
> They pass'd, and many a Region dolorous,
> O'er many a Frozen, many a Fiery Alp,
> Rocks, Caves, Lakes, Fens, Bogs, Dens, and shades
> of death,
> A Universe of death.
>
> (614–22)

The topographical aspects of Hell defined, Milton returns to Satan, who has reached the gates of Hell. The corresponding sections in Book XI describe the trumpet blast that marks the end of the snynod in Heaven at which God has announced his plans and sent Michael on an embassy not only to drive Adam and Eve from the garden (ironically, also Satan's mission), but also to "reveal/To Adam what shall come in future days" (XI. 113–14). While Michael descends, the scene shifts to Adam and Eve in the garden, awakening to their fallen state and perceiving new signs of the blight that marks the landscape of loss that now prevails in Eden and the outside world.

Examination of the remaining sections of these books shows that the balanced structure continues, underlined by several verbal parallels that have doctrinal as well as structural significance. The concluding section of Book II presents Satan and Sin contemplating the falling away that has occurred, as Sin recollects her creation and undoing at

Satan's hands. She determines, despite her losses, to stand with Satan, expressing what is, ironically, the appropriate hierarchical formula as she opens the gates of Hell for his "escape":

> Thou art my Father, thou my Author, thou
> My being gav'st me; whom should I obey
> But thee, whom follow?
>
> (II. 864–66)

For a moment Satan hesitantly views the "Illimitable Ocean" of Chaos that is "without bound/Without dimension" (II. 892–93), then leaps into it to be buffeted by winds until finally

> a universal hubbub wild
> Of stunning sounds and voices all confus'd
> Borne through the hallow dark assaults his ear
> With loudest vehemence.
>
> (II. 951–54)

Confronting Chaos himself, Satan petitions for his aid. The "Anarch old" tells Satan of the inroads to his kingdom caused by Satan's fall and the concomitant creation of Hell to receive him, but in the end he agrees to help Satan, directing him upward toward the light. We last glimpse Satan winging toward the pendant world and the first glimmering light from Heaven.

Book XI opens with the prayers of Adam and Eve "wing'd for Heav'n." They fly upward, too,

> nor miss'd the way, by envious winds
> Blown vagabond or frustrate: in they pass'd
> Dimensionless through Heav'nly doors.
>
> (15–17)

Heard by the Son, they are brought in supplication before God. God expounds on the "dissolution wrought by Sin" on man's kingdom, yet He remains willing to receive their prayers for forgiveness. Thus Book XI begins where Book II had ended, though forgiveness supplants revenge (see Fig. 4).

Several of the basic relationships that exist between Books I and XII have been discussed by J. R. Watson in his essay on "Divine Providence and the Structure of *Paradise Lost*." Watson's examples support the basic point he wishes to make, that the design of Milton's epic correlates with the concept of God's scheme of eternal love and redemption. Further scrutiny of these books reveals many additional parallels woven by Milton into the fabric of his epic.

In large measure the books repeat each other in a reversing pattern, structurally providing a kind of mirror image, the preciseness of which, at times, suggests that Milton hoped to establish the pattern fairly forcefully in the outer framework of the poem, even though the reader could not perceive the sharp relationship except in retrospect.

The first verse paragraph of *Paradise Lost* is twenty-six lines long and accomplishes both the entry into the poem and the initial movement upward by means of its verbal emphasis on rising and soaring: "Sing . . . how the Heav'ns and Earth/Rose out of *Chaos*"; "aid . . . my advent'rous Song,/That with no middle flight intends to soar/Above th' Aonian Mount"; "What in me is dark/Illumine, what is low raise and support." Milton provides a counterpart to this passage in the closing verse paragraph of the poem. Itself also twenty-six lines, it concludes the action of the poem describing the descent of Adam and Eve from Eden and out of the world of the poem. Led by Michael "down the cliff" to the "subjected plain,"

> Some natural tears they dropp'd, but wip'd them soon;
> The World was all before them, where to choose

BOOK II

Satan, high on throne, opens debate with disclaimer against
    ENVY in Hell
Demonic Debate: Moloch for open war
        Belial: "ignoble ease and peaceful sloth"
        Mammon: make a heaven out of hell
        Beelzebub: revenge on God through man

Satan offers to reconnoiter
Trumpets
Fallen angels' activities; explore "blighted" topography of Hell
Satan on mission; reaches Hell's gates

Confrontation; Sin and Death defined
Sin opens gates "without dimension"
        Satan steps off into Chaos: "buffeted by winds";
        petitions Chaos for help.
        Satan flies upward toward the light.

BOOK XI

Prayers of Adam and Eve fly upward, "wing'd for Heaven";
        prayers not buffeted by "envious winds"; pass "dimensionless"
        through Heaven's gates
Christ petitions God for Man
Christ petitions God for man
God calls synod; declares decree
Orders Michael undertake embassy to man
Trumpets

Dawn in Eden; signs of blight; Adam and Eve discuss who first
        brought death into the world
Michael arrives in Paradise; tells them they must depart;
        Eve's lament; Adam's lament
While Eve sleeps, Adam sees vision of world (topography of loss)
Sin and Death defined historically
Enoch protests against "sword law"

Adam sees slothful "tents of wickedness"
God's revenge on sinful man: the flood
God remits IRE; establishes covenant in rainbow

Selected Parallels between Books II and XI
Figure 4

> Thir place of rest, and Providence thir guide:
> They hand in hand with wand'ring steps and slow,
> Through *Eden* took thir solitary way.
>   (XII. 645–49)

The opening paragraph of Book I leads up to a definition of the "cause" of the events that the epic will take up:

> Say first, for Heav'n hides nothing from thy view
> Nor the deep Tract of Hell, say first what cause
> Mov'd our Grand Parents in that happy State,
> Favour'd of Heav'n so highly, to fall off
> From thir Creator, and transgress his Will
> For one restraint, Lords of the World besides?
>   (I. 27–32)

This passage, which includes, incidentally, another example of circular style in lines 27–28, anticipates the penultimate paragraph of Book XII, which defines the "effect" of Eve's role in God's total scheme of things. After Adam's vision of the future, he returns to Eve, finding her newly awakened and secure in the consolation that

> though all by mee is lost,
> Such favor I unworthy am voutsaf't,
> By mee the Promis'd Seed shall all restore.
>   (XII. 621–23)

While Adam received intelligence of the future from Michael, Eve has been calmed by "gentle Dreams. . . . Portending good," which have assured her of her role in man's ultimate restoration. As Eve awakens to a full knowledge of her new state (XII. 610–23), so in Book I has Satan awakened, and with

> baleful eyes
> That witness'd huge affliction and dismay
> Mixt with obdúrate pride and steadfast hate:
> At once as far as Angels' ken he views
> The dismal Situation waste and wild.
>   (I. 56–60)

But whereas Satan rests in "obdurate pride and steadfast hate," Eve responds with "spirits composed" and "meek submission" (XII. 597–97). As Satan raises his head, we recognize his determination to pursue evil and thus witness an infernal genesis, the result of which will be the "new beginning" that the close of Book XII heralds.

The balanced, reversing pattern persists clearly in the opening dialogue between Satan and Beelzebub and the closing discussion between Michael and Adam. In each the speakers define the implications of the situation at which they have arrived. In Book I Beelzebub replies to his leader's initial exhortations with words of anguish and despair:

> What can it then avail though yet we feel
> Strength undiminisht, or eternal being
> To undergo eternal punishment?
> (I. 153–55)

In Book XII Adam admits to being "greatly instructed" and "greatly in peace of thought" as a result of the vision he has been provided by Michael of the future of man (cf. XII. 552–73). Against the "dreadful deeds" of war that Beelzebub recalls as having lost the rebels their place in Heaven (I. 130–36), Adam reaffirms that he now understands how man will gain his "highest victory" by obedience and will subvert the "worldly strong"

> with good
> Still overcoming evil, and by small
> Accomplishing great things.
> (XII. 565–67)

Beelzebub fears "eternal punishment" at the hand of the Conqueror whom he must "now/Of force believe Almighty," but Adam sees that Death will be merely the "Gate of Life"

> Taught this by his example whom I now
> Acknowledge my Redeemer ever blest.
>   (XII. 572–73)

Adam's acceptance elicits from Michael the assurance that if Adam adds faith to his new knowledge, he may

> leave this Paradise, but shalt possess
> A paradise within . . . happier far.
>   (XII. 586–87)

Adam has lost an external, physical paradise but has gained the means to achieve a paradise of the mind far more secure and rewarding. In pointing out this aspect of his new state, Michael adds further assurance to Adam's resolution, and Milton may tacitly remind us that Satan had sought to exhort Beelzebub in very similar terms, though for different ends:

> What though the field be lost?
> All is not lost; the unconquerable Will,
> And study of revenge, immortal hate,
> And courage never to submit or yeild:
> And what is else not to be overcome?
>   (I. 105–9)

The reversing pattern continues emphatically in Adam's "celebration of the redemption":

> O goodness infinite, goodness immense!
> That all this good of evil shall produce,
> And evil turn to good.
>   (XII. 469–71)

The celebration accurately reverses Satan's statement of the program of evil he will follow:

> If then his Providence
> Out of our evil seek to bring forth good,
> Our labor must be to pervert that end,
> And out of good still to find means of evil.
>   (I. 162–65)

Almost as if in response to the implications of Satan's program, Michael surveys the effects of evil through the history of man only to affirm God's power ultimately "to bring forth fruits of Joy and eternal Bliss" (XII. 551).

A summary of the events thus far described in these books might look something like this:

	Book I (opening 191 lines)
1–26	"Rising" into poem's lofty matter
27–56	In Satan the "cause"
57–83	Satan awakens to his fallen state
84–127	Satan on the "unconquerable will"
128–56	Beelzebub on "dreadful deeds" of the past
157–91	Satan outlines demonic plan: evil from good

	Book XII (closing 183 lines)
466–84	Adam: "O goodness infinite"
485–551	Michael summarizes history; affirms God's plan to bring good from evil
552–53	Adam perceives how small things lead to great
574–94	Michael defines the "paradise within"
594–609	Eve awakens to her new state
610–23	In Eve the "effects"
624–49	"Descent" from world of poem

In the central section of Books I and XII, large elements balance each other, though it must be admitted that the details reflect one another more at random. The 470 lines

of Book I (192–662) following the dialogue between Beelzebub and Satan generally correspond with the 402 lines in
Book XII (63–465) that precede Adam's praise of the "infinite goodness" of God. These two large sections may in
turn each be divided into four segments that broadly match
their counterparts both in length and content. Following
his discussion with Beelzebub, Satan rouses himself from
the burning lake, surveys his new kingdom and comments
on his loss:

> Farewell happy Fields
> Where Joy for ever dwells. Hail horrors, hail
> Infernal world, and thou profoundest Hell
> Receive thy new Possessor.
>   (I. 249–52)

In this section, after comparing Satan to the sea-beast
Leviathan, Milton makes it clear that Satan rises again only
through "high permission of all-ruling Heaven" so that he

> enrag'd might see
> How all his malice serv'd but to bring forth
> Infinite goodness, grace and mercy shown
> On Man by him seduc't.
>   (I. 216–19)

Satan himself at least outwardly believes that it is "better
to reign in Hell, than serve in Heav'n" (263) and moves to
call his followers "to share with us then part/In this un-
happy Mansion" (267–68). Beelzebub urges Satan on in his
resolve to reassemble his forces, proclaiming

> Leader of those Armies bright,
> Which but th' Omnipotent none could have foiled,
> If once they hear that voice, thir liveliest pledge
> Of hope in fears and dangers, heard so oft
> In worst extremes, and on the perilous edge
> Of battle when it rag'd, in all assaults

Thir surest signal, they will soon resume
New courage and revive, though now they lie
Groveling and prostrate on yon Lake of Fire,
As we erewhile, astounded and amaz'd;
No wonder, fall'n such a pernicious highth.
(I. 272–82)

The whole section (192–282 = 90 lines) corresponds with a passage of equal length in Book XII (375–495), which begins with Adam's joyous response to Michael's promise of the Messiah. Compare Adam's speech, for example, with that of Beelzebub just quoted:

O Prophet of glad tidings, finisher
Of utmost hope! now clear I understand
What oft my steadfast thoughts have searcht in vain,
Why our great expectation should be call'd
The seed of Woman: Virgin Mother, Hail,
High in the love of Heav'n, yet from my Loins
Thou shalt proceed, and from thy Womb the Son
Of God most High; So God with man unites.
Needs must the Serpent now his capital bruise
Expect with mortal pain: say where and when
Thir fight, what stroke shall bruise the Victor's heel.
(XII. 375–85)

Both Beelzebub and Adam speak of the warfare between good and evil, both misconceiving the true nature of the struggle; both address their companion as the bearer of good tidings or the voice "of hope in fears and dangers." Of virtually the same length, the speeches contrast with each other as Beelzebub appropriately considers how fallen they are from "such a pernicious highth," unconsciously implying in "pernicious" the death they have gained, while Adam's speech concerns itself with man's ascent toward "God most High" and the new life that promises.

Michael replies to Adam's praise by explaining the true nature of the warfare between Christ and Satan. He describes the Crucifixion and Resurrection, the harrowing of

Hell and the work of the disciples who "All Nations . . . shall teach . . . So in his seed all Nations shall be blest" (446–50). Michael concludes with the promise that at Judgment

> the Earth
> Shall all be Paradise, far happier place
> Than this of *Eden,* and far happier days.
> (463–65)

These lines are a distant echo of Satan's statement in Book I, "The mind is its own place, and in itself/Can make a Heav'n of Hell, a Hell of Heav'n" and his affirmation "Better to reign in Hell, than serve in Heav'n" (254–55; 263). In this section of Book I, as I have indicated, Milton compares Satan to Leviathan, a type of evil related to Isaiah's prophecy (27: 1) that the Lord "shall slay the dragon that is in the sea," and makes it clear that Satan rises only by God's permission. In the corresponding section of Book XII Michael foretells the Resurrection and harrowing of Hell in a lengthy passage that contrasts with the description of Satan's rising from the burning lake:

> so he dies,
> But soon revives, Death over him no power
> Shall long usurp; ere the third dawning light
> Return, the Stars of Morn shall see him rise
> Out of his grave, fresh as the dawning light,
> Thy ransom paid, which Man from death redeems,
> His death for Man.
> (XII. 419–25)

Here as elsewhere the repetition serves to put into proper perspective the new life offered man to replace that lost as a result of evil regenerate from the flames of Hell.

The second segment begins in Book I with the Vallombrosa image and continues for 239 lines with Satan's unconsciously ironic and paradoxical exhortation that his followers "awake, arise, or be forever fall'n" (I. 330), and the great catalogue, rich with Old Testament allusion, of the fallen angels. Against it, in Book XII, Milton sets a passage only slightly shorter (203 lines), in which he chronicles the Old Testament heroes, Moses, Aaron, Joshua, Solomon, and David, the human adversaries of the Satanic crew. This passage (XII. 171–374) also contains the discussion between Michael and Adam of the true relationship between law and faith, a discussion not strictly balanced against a similar passage in Book I, though we may be meant to read the whole catalogue of devils as a description of the evils of faithlessness on the part of the tribes of man who turn from the law to worship alien deities. Milton imbues the catalogues with historical and typological complexity by building both around nine major figures who roughly correspond to each other as antagonist and protagonist. Against the demons Moloch, Chemos, Baalim, Astoreth, Thammuz, Dagon, Rimmion, Osiris, and Belial described in Book I, Milton places the Worthies, Abraham, Isaac, Jacob, Joseph, Aaron, Moses, Josiah, David, and Solomon. The link between Solomon and Moloch is specifically made by Milton in Book I when he reminds his reader that it was Moloch who led "the wiser heart/Of Solomon . . . by fraud to build/His Temple right against the Temple of God" (400–402). At the other end of the catalogue, Milton links Abraham and Belial in Book I by reference to the destruction of Sodom (II. 500ff.). Other links are more general, but at the core of each group are the relationships between Aaron and Moses and the false Gods associated with the captivity and later flight from Egypt. As we would expect from their common Old Testament frame of reference, both segments contain many of the same allusions. Particularly noteworthy, however, is the relationship between the extended reference to the passage of the Red Sea (I. 304–11) and the destruction of "Busiris and his Memphian Chivalry," a passage that looks forward to the narrative account in Book XII of the flight from Egypt (190–212).

The account in Book XII repeats some key words and phrases to point up the relationship. Note, for example, the use in both passages of the adjective "sojourners" to describe the Jews in captivity, and the comparison of their prospect of the fallen troops

> who beheld
> From the safe shore thir floating Carcasses
> And broken Chariot Wheels,
>
> (309–11)

with the description in XII of how God

> looking forth will trouble all the Host
> And craze thir Chariot wheels.
>
> (209–10)

In this same section of Book XII, Milton describes the "darksome Cloud of Locusts" called down on Pharaoh by Moses, a swarm of insects that will provide a "palpable darkness" like "the palpable obscure" Milton associates with Hell (II. 406). The reference to the plague of locusts has appeared previously in Book I (338–41) to describe the fallen Angels rising at Satan's exhortation:

> Yet to thir General's Voice they soon obey'd
> Innumerable. As when the potent Rod
> Of *Amram's* Son in *Egypt's* evil day
> Wav'd round the Coast, up call'd a pitchy cloud
> Of *Locusts*, warping on the Eastern Wind,
> That o'er the Realm of impious *Pharaoh* hung
> Like Night, and darken'd all the Land of *Nile.*
>
> (I. 337–43)

Across the surface of the poem, then, the great demonic antagonists are set against their adversaries in a historical pattern that reemphasizes God's control and the providential nature of his plan.[30]

The third and final section of Book I (lines 522–798) corresponds to the opening one-hundred-and-fifty-one lines of Book XII. Following the catalogue of the fallen in Book I, Milton describes at length the rising of the hordes, the vastness of whose number makes Satan's heart distend "with pride" (572). Though Satan has earlier called his followers to "awake, arise, or be for ever fall'n" (330), the demons approach him "with looks/Downcast and damp" (522–23). It remains necessary for him to raise "thir fainting courage" by means of "high words, that bore/Semblance of worth . . . and dispelled thir fears" (528–30). Against this Milton places a briefer passage in Book XII (111–70), in which Michael describes for Adam how "a Nation from one faithful man" will spring from the loins of Abraham, whom God called to rise and go forth into "a land unknown" (134). Satan's response to the rising of his legions is a harangue urging "war/Open or understood," even though he has admitted an unconscious contradiction of his own position by claiming earlier that his forces remain ready to fight again, since "who overcomes/By force, hath overcome but half his foe" (cf. I. 622–62). How different in tone is the dialogue set in the corresponding position in Book XII, which takes place between Adam and Michael on the subject of right reason. Adam has responded emphatically against the description of the building of the Tower of Babel:

30. For the mythic significance of the exodus image, see John Shawcross, *"Paradise Lost* and the Theme of Exodus," *Milton Studies II* (1970), pp. 3–26: "Exodus as myth epitomizes (or typifies) the ritual that must constantly be undertaken to achieve the dream of reunion with the godhead. . . . The ritual involved in exodus is a constant forward motion through successive stages of action and time, each a beginning again, an involvement in false security and error, and a removal from that involvement to a period of trial and purgation as things begin again. It is not cyclic. The mythic quest is thus mankind's constant striving forward to its dream through the ritual of exodus . . . (pp. 5–6).

> to God his Tower intends
> Siege and defiance: Wretched man!
>
>   (XII. 73–74)

Only to have Michael inform him:

> Justly thou abhorr'st
> . . . .
>   yet know withal,
> Since thy original lapse, true Liberty
> Is lost, which always with right Reason dwells
> Twinn'd, and from her hath no dividual being:
> Reason in man obscur'd, or not obey'd,
> Immediately inordinate desires
> And upstart Passions catch the Government
> From Reason, and to servitude reduce
> Man till then free.
>
>   (XII. 79, 82–90)

What an appropriate comment, in retrospect, on the militant speech of the tyrant Satan, who has lost all rationality as a result of his "original lapse" and who, like his followers, finds himself caught in a maze of contradictory statement and hopeless debate.

Finally, as Adam's outcry stems from his reaction to Michael's description of Nimrod and the building of the Tower of Babel (XII. 13–62), so the immediate response of the fallen to Satan's exhortation in Book I is, of course, the building of Pandemonium. The account of the building of Pandemonium itself contains a reference to Babel and to the rebels' "hurling defiance toward the Vault of Heav'n" (I. 669). Beyond this, the description of "the veins of liquid fire/Sluic'd from the Lake" (I. 700–701) by the fallen angels and poured into molds to build Pandemonium seems clearly related to the passage early in Book XII telling how Nimrod's crew,

Marching from *Eden* towards the West, shall find
The Plain, wherein a black bituminous gurge
Boils out from under ground, the mouth of Hell;
Of Brick, and of that stuff they cast to build
A City and Tow'r, whose top may reach to Heav'n.
                    (XII. 40–44)

The account of the building of Babel ends with God's sending down a confusion of tongues on the builders, produc-
ing a "hubbub strange" (XII. 60) that echoes the beelike
swarming of the fallen angels into the new-built citadel and
their reduction in size "to smallest forms" so that they may
be accommodated in the edifice (I. 768–69). The reduction
itself may plausibly be likened to the diminishing of Adam's
sight at the beginning of Book XII, which necessitates that
Michael narrate the events I have just been discussing.
These sections of Books I and XII may be schematized as
in figure 5.

I doubt that all the parallels between Books I and XII
have been set forth. It is one of the tributes to Milton's
particular genius that the parallels are so complex and numerous and yet so unobtrusive. One discovers more with
each reading, yet never feels impeded by the design. The
effect achieved by these parallels is difficult to determine,
however, especially since they have until recently remained
largely unnoticed. At most we are meant merely to sense
them (and in writing about them one should perhaps adopt
the devices of Moses ben Maimon and write an esoteric
analysis of an esoteric subject).[31] But the pronounced pattern at the center of the poem is certainly to be seen as a
direct sign of God's perfection and eternality at the center
of all existence. The pattern in the opening and closing
books is probably intentionally elaborate because these
books form the outer ring of the circular composition.
They, too, provide an image of the circular perfection of

31. Leo Strauss, *Persecution and the Art of Writing,* cited in n.10 above.

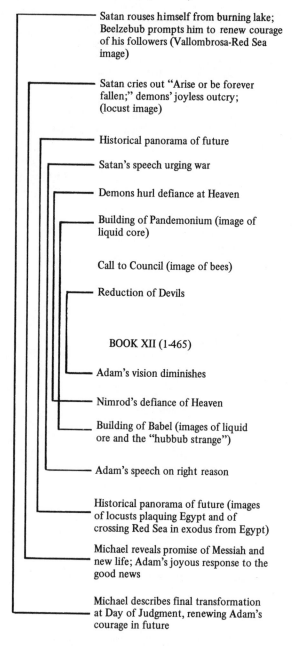

BOOK I (192-798)

Satan rouses himself from burning lake; Beelzebub prompts him to renew courage of his followers (Vallombrosa-Red Sea image)

Satan cries out "Arise or be forever fallen;" demons' joyless outcry; (locust image)

Historical panorama of future

Satan's speech urging war

Demons hurl defiance at Heaven

Building of Pandemonium (image of liquid core)

Call to Council (image of bees)

Reduction of Devils

BOOK XII (1-465)

Adam's vision diminishes

Nimrod's defiance of Heaven

Building of Babel (images of liquid ore and the "hubbub strange")

Adam's speech on right reason

Historical panorama of future (images of locusts plaquing Egypt and of crossing Red Sea in exodus from Egypt)

Michael reveals promise of Messiah and new life; Adam's joyous response to the good news

Michael describes final transformation at Day of Judgment, renewing Adam's courage in future

Schematized Sections of Books I and XII

Figure 5

the divine scheme that binds all together. Like a poetic empyrean they display the ultimate form of things as we know them. As Book I impels us forward on the great arc of evil, so XII circles away from the treachery and loss that comprise Satan's version of Eden; the pagan images of the sphere of fire give way to the providential images of the sphere of history and to the certainty of final rest. The descent from Eden is a rising, as surely as the initial rising marks out the lines of the great falling away. Just so, the pattern makes it clearer by specific echoes and redefinitions that, while Satan may have appeared to be the hero throughout the early books, the reversals and substitutions depicted in Books XI and XII emphasize the truly heroic character of Adam and Eve. Their overall humility and patience are the only fit and reasonable response to their situation, less "glamorous" than Satan's swashbuckling militancy, no doubt, but eminently more sensible.

3

The Interpenetration
of Time and Space

If Milton shaped *Paradise Lost* in the way I have been describing, he risked creating a design the sheer weight of which could endanger the vitality of his poem. If the circular design became too obvious, the effect would be static rather than dynamic. Though conceptually Milton might have relished the apparent similarity between his dilemma and that of the Divinity, who assured man of his freedom but set him within the confines of a predetermined scheme, artistically he would have recognized the need for great care to avoid restrictiveness. All writers face such structural problems in the course of their work. For Milton, however, the problem was extreme. The shape must be pervasive, but it must not become a formula. Speaking generally of this kind of difficulty, Kermode points out that "the concords books arrange between beginning, middle, and end" cannot provide too precise a shape to life without becoming "the opium of the people," for

> fictions too easy we call "escapist"; we want them not only to console but to make discoveries of the hard truth here and now, in the middest. . . . The books which seal off the long perspectives, which sever us from our losses, which represent

the world of potency as a world of act, these are the books
which, when the drug wears off, go on to the dump with the
other empty bottles. Those that continue to interest us move
through time to an end, an end we must sense even if we
cannot know it; they live in change, until, which is never, *as* and
is are one.[1]

These remarks go beyond matters of mere aesthetic deco-
rum and artistic probability to touch the essence of our
imaginative being. That Milton's sensibility could accept
without difficulty the relevance one to the other of spatial
and temporal concepts I have mentioned. The larger question of how the closed form of *Paradise Lost* avoids the
dangers of becoming primarily static, of how Milton's
poem opens up rather than seals off "the long perspectives" to our imagination by means of a complex temporal
awareness will be, in large part, the concern of the remainder of this book.

The actual physical structure of *Paradise Lost* lay unobtrusively, like "the treasures of time," just beneath the surface
of the poem for almost three centuries before rising to our
view. The success of the anagogical plan, in this case, may
have been partially the result of a glittering surface that
would satisfy most "enquirers." But Milton also provided
for the keeping of his structural secret and the avoidance
of an overbearing design in a number of other ways, such
as the direct sequential parallels or oppositions we find
between books. Recall, for example, the well-known parallels established between the antagonist Satan in Book II
and the Son in Book III. Of particular interest to the present study, however, is the way Milton introduced various
temporal perspectives to imbue his poem with the qualities
of movement and change. Like the circle, the poem returns
upon itself only to turn again, embracing all historical time
in the great circle of eternity. As the old, closed order of

1. *The Sense of an Ending,* pp. 178–79.

the Aristotelian-Ptolemaic universe had been pierced by the shafts of infinitude, at once spatial and temporal, so the world of *Paradise Lost* mirrors the interpenetration of space and time. Confined within time and space, men can see beyond their limits to a point at which being and becoming are one and "all in all" with God. The apocalyptic perspective is vast. The end in view provides at once comfort and continuing perplexity.[2]

To achieve this sense Milton employs a number of patterns that often work simultaneously to create a kind of temporal metabolism. Of primary force quite naturally is the chronological pattern that underlies the events of the poem. Event follows event in a definite, knowable pattern at once consistent with the historical data of Milton's story and consonant with the temporal quality of a work of literature. In terms of the mechanics of time as Milton would have understood them, the chronological sense of the flow of events in sequence was to be distinguished from a more dramatic recognition of the way certain events shift out of the precise, knowable sequence to disrupt or reconstitute the pattern. To designate our apprehension of sequential time, the word *chronos* is normally applied. Dramatic time is understood by the term *kairos*, suggesting the sense of crisis in which significant events impinge upon the slow duration of time from one moment to the next.[3] Throughout *Paradise Lost* Milton establishes a tension between *chronos* and *kairos*, between sequential and dramatic time. In terms of strict sequence, for example, Milton's story begins with the Exaltation of the Son, an event not actually described in the narrative until Book V. Milton delays depicting this event, shaping time

2. For aspects of the apocalyptic in Milton, see Leland Ryken, *The Apocalyptic Vision in* Paradise Lost (Ithaca, N.Y. 1970).
3. Cf. James Barr, *Biblical Words for Time,* "Studies in Biblical Theology" (London, 1962).

dramatically by beginning *in medias res,* as Satan raises his head from the burning lake determined to persist in evil. The epic formula for beginning allows Milton to make extended use of flashback through the central books of his poem to recapitulate the events that have come before, and allows him to warp time to his own ends, providing in the middle of his poem a statement of the major event, the victory over Sin, that embraces all time. Both techniques serve to reshape time and occasionally to charge it with the electricity of crisis. Milton thus detaches certain moments from the flow of *chronos* and provides them with the importance of *kairos,* the time *when:* the time *when* Satan raises his head in Hell; the time *when* Adam falls; the time *when* Christ dies; the time *when* Apocalypse ends the whole experiment in time. Overriding both these aspects of time is a more mythically understood element that involves our sense of the organic and creative, while providing an antidote to what Eliade calls the "terror of history," to its irrevocableness and its insistent sense that all things must end. Both *chronos* and *kairos* posit what is basically a rectilinear concept of time. By moments of crisis the line of time may be broken, disrupted, or redirected, but the basic flow remains forward toward an end. By emphasizing a rectilinear concept of time, Milton was following orthodox Christian thinking about the events of history. Augustine had argued against the Neoplatonists and the Stoics, for example, denying the former's conception of time as flux in which there is nothing real or decisive, and the latter's sense of history as consisting of endlessly recurring cycles of events. For Augustine, historical time has a beginning, and events, following one another in a straight line, occur once for all. Time is thus dramatically conceived; its acts decide man's future. The central historical events, of course, are the Crucifixion and Resurrection. In these events history reaches its *kairos* and, in a sense, its end. There will be movement forward, to be sure, but the divine plan has been made manifest and the goal is in sight.[4]

Milton does not really alter this view of history in his manipulation of time. Though he does not follow Augustine in his belief that time begins with the Creation, Milton essentially sees history as dramatic and charges events with potency. But he also employs a cyclical sense of time. It is evident in the seasonal round that gives promise of return and renewal. More important, it is there, so to speak, to provide an aesthetic solution to the Christian paradox of time and eternity by which Milton could dynamically relate an eternal being to a world of changing events. With something of the quality of mythic time, the cyclical primarily serves a cosmic purpose in Milton. Its promise softens the harsh line of irrevocability as time seems to "fold back" on itself and remind us of larger prospects than the diurnal. The span of one's life may be brief, an act in that span may be irrevocable, but there is a larger expanse of time that we feel envelops and protects and redeems us.[5] Milton achieves this sense of time both by means of the overall structure of the poem as I have described it, and by imagery that embraces past, present, and future, seemingly emphasizing the repetition of events and situations, but carefully drawing the differences in terms of God's plan. It is by means of imagery of this type that Eve anticipates Pandora or Ceres, but also Mary; it is by means of this type of image that Adam anticipates Christ as well as the average suffering, agonizing, indomitable man of all ages. The sense of prolonged time that turns on itself, perfecting through

4. See *Confessions,* Bk. XI, and *The City of God,* XI–XII.
5. Consult Miss Colie's essay on "Paradox and Structure in *Paradise Lost."* Any account of mythic time ought to be read in light of Ernst Cassirer's excellent study in *The Philosophy of Symbolic Forms,* vol. 2, "Mythical Thought," trans. Ralph Manheim (New Haven, Conn., 1955). Of particular interest to my investigation is chap. 2: "Foundations of a Theory of Mythical Forms. Space, Time, and Number," pp. 83–151.

change, is different from Stoic notions of the cyclical because of its emphasis forward toward completion; it is different from Neoplatonic concepts because of its insistence
on history rather than fable. It is of this world and yet
cosmic, as it reflects the scope of God's atemporal, perfect
being that has neither beginning nor end. The effect ultimately is, as Albert Cirillo has said in another context,

> that of a double time scheme whereby events that are being
> expressed in temporal terms—in sequential action—are simul-
> taneously occurring in the eternal present which is the central
> setting of the poem. The temporal, in this view, is the meta-
> phor for the eternal, and time in its dual aspect becomes a basis
> for structure.[6]

The sense of mythic or cosmic time hence bridges the great
gulf in the world of Milton's poem as in the world of actuality between man's temporal and God's eternal being. This
last, atemporal element, we can know only mysteriously in
the most fleeting moments of cognition in the actual world.
In *Paradise Lost* Milton embodies this kind of time, first of
all, by means of simple discursive reference, as when God
speaks of His entire plan, contemplating the fall of Satan:

>   I can repair
> That detriment, if such it be to lose
> Self-lost, and in a moment will create
> Another World, out of one man a Race
> Of men innumerable, there to dwell,
> Not here, till by degrees of merit rais'd
> They open to themselves at length the way

6. "Noon-Midnight and the Temporal Structure of *Paradise Lost*," *ELH* 29 (1962):
372–73. I do not think that all of Cirillo's midnight and noon time designations
are entirely accurate. For example, it is not clear that Satan begins falling from
Heaven at noon (see n. 11 below); and Milton seems to be explicit about the time
when Satan puts the evil dream into Eve's mind. Milton's reference is to nine
o'clock, not midnight. Cirillo's original essay, nevertheless, well argues the general notions of symbolic time in *Paradise Lost* and reinforces analyses of the
complex design of the epic.

Up hither, under long obedience tri'd,
And Earth be chang'd to Heav'n, and Heav'n to Earth,
One Kingdom, Joy and Union without end.
                              (VII. 152–61)

But the poem also achieves something of the mystical sense of eternity, of course, through its poetry and through the occasional metaphoric achievement by which man glimpses time from his vantage point in history and simultaneously from that of preceding and following ages. We participate on several levels of reality. We are at once made aware of our presence watching the poet creating his epic, a task that itself stands in direct relation to the imaginative worlds being described and being enacted. We have a cosmic vantage point, aware of ourselves both in and out of time, participating with the creator in his work, hastening onward toward a finite goal within the infinite circle of the creative imagination, seeking a season, in Wallace Stevens's phrase, of "major weather."

The chronological lines that underly the entire epic are at times quite pronounced. Such is the case with Books IV and IX. These books do not maintain the *reversing* pattern of the other books. The repetitive emphasis here is strictly chronological. Book IX repeats events similar to those of Book IV in much the same sequence and thereby provides something of the mysterious quality of having previously experienced a set of actions, perhaps, but not the sense of inversion. God's shaping (and controlling) hand is less evident in the structure of events in these books. It is as if Milton were attempting here to suggest man's actual freedom within the framework of God's omniscience. The chronological emphasis depicts the day-to-day activities of Adam and Eve, free to choose among a range of possibilities. In this sense Book IX is a reenactment, an ironic fulfillment of the garden drama presented in Book IV.

Milton begins Book IV with a brief dramatic outcry against the impending danger that faces man in the guise of Satan:

> O for that warning voice, which he who saw
> Th' *Apocalypse,* heard cry in Heav'n aloud,
> Then when the Dragon, put to second rout,
> Came furious down to be reveng'd on men,
> *Woe to the inhabitants on Earth!* that now,
> While time was, our first Parents had been warn'd
> The coming of thir secret foe, and scap'd
> Haply so scap'd his mortal snare,
> (IV. 1–8)

and introduces Satan, "how first inflam'd with rage," who stands atop Mount Niphates and scans the universe, in torment at the Hell he finds within him. As "conscience wakes despair," Satan addresses the Sun with hatred, uttering an ironic praise of light that both reflects the hymn to heavenly light with which Milton opened Book III and anticipates Satan's soliloquy on his return to Eden in Book IX. Addressing the Sun, Satan finds its light a hateful reminder of his former heavenly state, from which "bright eminence" he fell because he "sdein'd subjection, and thought one step higher/Would set" him highest (IV. 50–51). Satan's contemplation of the celestial order leads him to consider the true nature of his former position in Heaven and recognize that he cannot shift the blame for his fall from himself:

> Hadst thou the same free Will and Power to stand?
> Thou hadst: whom hast thou then or what to accuse,
> But Heav'n's free Love dealt equally to all?
> (IV. 66–68)

He realizes that he himself is Hell, that for him there is "no place/Left for Repentance" (79–80), that with each step he sinks lower into the mire of damnation. The soliloquy closes with his resolve to seek solace through the subversion of man. Milton describes the external disfiguration that Satan's troubled thoughts produce in him, an alteration that the angel Uriel observes from his place in the Sun and reports to the angelic guardian of Eden. Having ended his lament, Satan fares onward to the border of Eden. The entire movement is complete in 130 lines, a passage considerably shorter than its counterpart in Book IX, though the soliloquy itself is almost precisely the length of Satan's speech at the opening of Book IX. Book IX opens with an elaborate invocation in which the "warning voice" of the poet proclaims the imminent danger that will manifest itself in tragedy. The warning is followed by a discussion of heroic song and the task of the poet, a passage that has no counterpart in Book IV (IX. 13–47). Returning to his narrative, Milton describes the night of Satan's return to Eden, his decision to hide himself within the snake, and the renewed grief that wells up within him at the prospect of his loss, which the sight of Eden's beauty brings him (48–98). The 80-line lament that follows develops along very much the same lines as the 82-line soliloquy in Book IV. The earth bathed in the light of the stars reminds Satan of his former state in Heaven, where God's light extended to all, and leads him to recognize that

> the more I see
> Pleasures about me, so much more I feel
> Torment within me, as from the hateful siege
> Of contraries; all good to me becomes
> Bane.
>
> (IX. 119–23)

He recalls here, as he had in Book IV, his debt of leadership owed to those who followed him in revolt. As this thought made repentance seem treachery in Book IV, here it inspires Satan to new glory, to reign "sole among/Th' infernal Powers" (135–36). At the same time, as Satan contemplates the serpent, his "foul descent" from his former eminence once more torments him through the need to "incarnate and imbrute" himself in the bestial essence (163–66). Satan rationalizes the situation by proclaiming "who aspires must down as low/As high he soar'd" (169–70) and renews his resolve to be revenged on God through man. With this conclusion, Satan enters the serpent to await the dawn.

The soliloquy in Book IV is followed by an elaborate description of Eden as Satan fares onward toward the garden. The description establishes the vital yet timeless quality of Eden and emphasizes in particular its "odorous" essence that "so entertain's" Satan on his journey toward Paradise. He enters the garden itself and perches, like a cormorant, on the Tree of Life. In the following passage Milton describes Paradise briefly and assures us that it is more exquisite than

> that fair field
> Of *Enna*, where *Prosperin* gath'ring flow'rs
> Herself a fairer Flow'r by gloomy *Dis*
> Was gather'd, which cost *Ceres* all that pain
> To seek her through the world.
> (IV. 268–72)

Against this background of beauty and wistful premonition, Adam and Eve enter, walking "hand in hand"

> the loveliest pair
> That ever since in love's embraces met.
> (IV. 321–22)

Their loveliness is so profound, indeed, that it causes Satan's speech to fail him momentarily. When he recovers himself he utters the dark soliloquy "O Hell! what do mine eyes with grief behold" (IV. 358–92), and in the shape of a lion, first, and then of a tiger "stalks . . . nearer to view his prey."

The comparable section of Book IX begins at line 192 with a very brief description of Eden at dawn:

> when all things that breathe
> From th' Earth's great Altar send up silent praise
> To the Creator, and his Nostrils fill
> With grateful Smell.
>
> (IX. 194–96)

The description itself serves to remind us of the much more elaborate and sensually precise description in Book IV, with its emphasis on the fragrance of the garden. In its brevity, however, it is in no way comparable to the longer passage, but the pace is quickening and Milton may mean to suggest something of the new tempo by the very brevity of this passage, which treats the praise of the Creator in so perfunctory a fashion. Adam and Eve join "thir vocal Worship to the Choir/Of Creatures wanting voice" (198–99) and then turn quickly to the business at hand and to the question of how best they "may ply/Thir growing work: for much thir work outgrew/The hands' dispatch of two Gard'ning so wide" (201–3). In a dialogue that has no counterpart in Book IV, Adam and Eve discuss separation, so that they may work more diligently and effectively to keep the garden from overgrowing. The psychological implications of Adam and Eve's dialogue have been fully discussed by other scholars, and their evaluations need not concern us here. In point of contrast, the dialogue naturally provides the discordant note of gentle quarrel that is nowhere to be found in the initial view of Paradise. After much debate, darkened by ominous overtones, Eve

> from her Husband's hand her hand
> Soft . . . withdrew,
>
> (IX. 385–86)

and "betook her to the Groves." Eve is once again described in the context of the flowers of her garden, now just

before her temptation, when she goes forth like Ceres in
her prime and as she ties up the drooping stalks,

> Herself, though fairest unsupported Flow'r,
> From her best prop so far, and storm so nigh.
> (IX. 432–33)

Once again Satan stands in awe of her beauty, as if "ab-
stracted"

> From his own evil, and for the time [remains]
> Stupidly good, of enmity disarm'd.
> (IX. 464–65)

When he finds his voice, it is to reaffirm his bitter resolve
in spite of the beauty he beholds, which has with "sweet/
Compulsion thus transported to forget/What hither
brought" him to Eden, that is, "hate, not love, nor hope/Of
Paradise for Hell." Once enclosed in the body of the serpent, he "curl'd many a wanton wreath in sight of *Eve*, To
lure her Eye" and draw her closer to him.

Up to this point, it seems to me, the parallels between
Books IV and IX are quite exact enough to support the
claim that Milton has consciously reworked the materials of
one book in terms of the tone of another. As I have said,
we have in Book IX the mysterious sense of seeing something over again. The repetition of the pattern prepares us
for the test that could have occurred earlier. In other
words, we are allowed to sense, if only intuitively, that in
both instances—in Book IV as well as in IX—the possibility
of evil exists. In Book IV, of course, it leads only to an
interrupted dream of evil. In IX that dream becomes reality
and thus reduces to dream for all time the former reality of
innocence. We attain a mythic feeling in relation to the
story Milton narrates, but it is the generalized myth of loss
pervading our being that we take away. What Milton presents us with, however, is the specificity of the dramatized
incident, the *peripeteia* or sudden reversal that grows out of

the day-by-day pattern of repeated event: what is normally, what has been, what is, what might have been. All are caught by the relentless flow of event, the historical chronology of being that denies finally the essence of intemporality. Things repeat themselves, and yet they do not. The specifics lead to mythologization, the generalizing tendency we brood over in abstraction as Satan broods over the beauty of Eve before undertaking to destroy that beauty forever.

The second half of these books portrays the difference between what is and what might have been. The second half of Book IV may be said to begin with Adam's speech to Eve in which he defines the purpose of the Tree of Knowledge and reminds her of the prohibition against eating its fruit. Eve responds affirmatively and then recounts her recollections of the first moments of her being. In her description of the initial, narcissistic reaction to her reflection in the lake, we are, of course, meant to have a presentiment of her fall before the flattery of Satan in Book IX. Throughout this scene in Book IV, Satan has watched the majestic couple as they strolled through the garden. Now, having heard all that is necessary for his ends, "his proud step he scornful turn'd,/But with sly circumspection, and began/Through wood, through waste, o'er hill, o'er dale to roam" (536–38). The scene shifts to Gabriel with the angelic guard, to whom Uriel reports how he met Satan "at highth of Noon" and later watched as Satan was transformed "with passions foul" (564–71). From the angelic guard Milton returns to Adam and Eve and creates around them at nightfall a beautiful scene of matrimonial concord and perfect harmony. After some discourse about the reason for the night stars, in which Eve is properly schooled by means of Adam's superior reason, the two offer spontaneous prayer to God for his creation, and hand-in-hand pass on "to thir blissful Bower" (690). The innocence and goodness of their "adoration pure" causes the poet to offer his hymn to wedded love:

Hail wedded Love, mysterious Law, true source
Of human offspring, sole propriety,
In Paradise of all things common else.
(750–52)

At nine o'clock Satan finds Eve asleep and squats by her side in the shape of a toad, putting into her mind the dream of temptation, which she will relate to Adam the next morning. The angelic guards find Satan "close at the ear of *Eve*" and return with him to Gabriel. There follows a near-struggle only prevented when God hangs his celestial scales in the sky to deter Satan from a battle, hopeless for him to undertake.

The second half of Book IX begins with Satan's flattery of Eve, in the course of which he redefines for her the Tree of Knowledge and begins to subvert in her mind the prohibition against eating its fruit. At first Eve remains unconvinced, and finds the visit to the tree "fruitless" for her, but Satan's arguments gradually undermine her resolve. Noon approaches; she fixes upon the apple and, as in her dream in Book IV, is beguiled by its aroma. With praise for the tree and growing intoxication, she eats the apple. In so doing she defines her death in an act that may be seen to be the tragic counterpart to the description of her birth in Book IV. At this point, Satan in the guise of the serpent slinks away "for *Eve*/Intent now wholly on her taste, naught else/Regarded." Book IX lacks a scene comparable to that in IV in which Uriel warns Gabriel of Satan's presence in the garden, unless one sees Eve's encounter with Adam, which precedes his resolve to fall with her, as serving the function of a warning to him of the presence of evil in the garden, providing him one last chance to salvage innocence from death. But Adam decides to fall with Eve and eats the apple. There follows a scene of lust and discord that is both the immediate effect of the transgression and the antithesis to the blissful concord we witnessed in Book IV. Against the concord of "wedded love," we now experience absolute discord of "weak indulgence." Intoxicated and swimming in mirth, Adam praises Eve and the exactness of her taste, crying out

> never did thy Beauty since the day
> I saw thee first and wedded thee, adorn'd
> With all perfections, so inflame my sense
> With ardor to enjoy thee, fairer now
> Than ever, bounty of this virtuous Tree.
> (IX. 1029–33)

So saying, "her hand he seiz'd," and led her to their bower where, finally exhausted by "amorous play," he falls asleep only to wake like

> the *Danite* strong
> *Herculean Samson* from the Harlot-lap
> Of *Philistean Delilah*, . . .
> Shorn of his strength.
> (IX. 1059–62)

The comparison itself recalls the earlier hymn to wedded love, in which Milton contrasted the original bliss of Edenic love with "the bought smile/Of Harlots, loveless, joyless, unindear'd,/Casual fruition" (IV. 765–67) so like the unfruitful feast following the Fall. Book IX closes on a note of discord that recalls the final scene in Book IV. In the latter, Satan flees "murmuring," having been weighed in God's scales and found wanting. Just so, Adam and Eve are reduced to verbal bitterness and "mutual accusation" at the close of Book IX.

Thus, the danger implicit in Book IV has been realized in IX. The evil that threatened the idyllic splendor has now eclipsed it in darkness. And as we look back over the events of the two books with a kind of anguish, tempered only by a more certain knowledge of the symmetry of God's own plan to bring good out of evil, we realize in justice to God that the darkness could easily have been dispersed by Adam and Eve. But the repetitive, linear pattern has served, as well, to emphasize the pattern of man's life. Within the grand circular schema of the other books, IV and IX provide an image of man's mortal line, the short span of his being embraced within the eternal providence of God. Emblematically, the combination reminds us of the hieroglyph of man's life, expressed for the Renaissance in the Greek letter theta, Θ, at once an image of death or *thanatos,* and the assurance of God's perfect, constant, eternal womb of love and life.[7]

The time schemes of *Paradise Lost* have been carefully worked out by Milton. Though they may occasionally seem indefinite, they are, I believe, quite precisely presented throughout the poem. Ultimately, of course, the poem refers to all time, indeed, moves beyond time. In reference to the immediate narrative present and past, Milton develops the chronology of his poem in accord both with verisimilitude and with symbolic interpretations of the Genesis story that he was heir to. The time span of events presented as occurring or having occurred in the poem is twenty-eight days. Although it may be worth noting in passing that Pythagorean numerology held twenty-eight to be the second perfect number—the number of the lunar month—more importantly, the period coincides with what Grant McColley calls the "second most influential interpretation" of the time-scheme of the Creation and Fall.[8]

7. Marjorie Hope Nicolson, p. 48. "If the Greek *chi* reminded man of the divine origin of the soul, another Greek character, theta Θ—a combination of circle and straight line, and the first letter of *Thanatos,* or Death—was his evidence of mortality." "Circles and right lines," as Browne said, "limit and close up all besides, and the mortal right-lined circle must conclude and shut up all" (*Hydriotaphia* IV. 45). God's symbol was the circle; man's the straight line.
8. Paradise Lost *and the Hexameral Tradition* (Chicago, 1940), p. 160. For details of McColley's time-scheme, see n. 12 below.

Let me briefly recount the twenty-eight-day pattern. The event that begins this chronological sequence is the Elevation of the Son (V. 600ff.). Generally speaking, this moment was not regarded by orthodox theologians as having occurred in time, not only because the Son was normally assumed to be coeternal with the Father, but also because time itself was generally considered on biblical and classical authority to have begun to be measured only at the Creation. But in *De Doctrina Christiana*, Milton clearly states that in his view time ought probably to be related to the Creation of the Son. Lawrence Stapleton notes the Miltonic distinction in his article on "Milton's Conception of Time":

> In order to appreciate Milton's careful and individual approach to the question, it is necessary to recall the sharp distinction between time and eternity which Christian tradition had promulgated. The adopted doctrine held, in accordance with Plato's teaching in the Timaeus, that time came into existence at the beginning of the world. Thus Augustine argues. . . . In Milton's discussion of the Son, and the justification for the view that the Son is not coeternal with the Father, we begin to see the novelty of Milton's approach to time . . . [and] it is abundantly clear that the generation of the Logos is the first event in time.[9]

Whereas nothing in *Paradise Lost* forces us to accept the conclusions of the *Christian Doctrine* in this regard, Milton's handling of the Elevation involves a definite sequence of events, from the prior existence of the angelic hierarchy to the later Elevation, and the resultant withdrawal at night of Satan to his stronghold in the North to raise rebellion. Before the Elevation there is nothing to suggest a state other than one of atemporal being. To be sure, the angels as a group must have been created prior to the Elevation, but Milton puts no emphasis on this fact, allowing the existence prior to the Exaltation of the Son to remain in the

---

9. *De Doctrina Christiana, Works* (1933), 14: 181, 189; Stapleton's article appears in the *Harvard Theological Review* 57 (1964): 9–21.

natural cloud of Heaven. If we accept the Elevation, therefore, as a chronological fact tallying with Milton's thinking in the *Christian Doctrine,* we must logically date that event as having occurred on the first "day" of the poem's chronological scheme.[10]

Satan withdraws at midnight. This, the second major occurence of the poem, initiates the action of the *second* day, in accordance with the evidence of the poem, which indicates that Milton follows the Hebrew custom of numbering the new day from dusk. Certainly in his description of the Creation, Milton follows this method as he specifically defines the days from dusk to dawn:

> Thus was the first Day Ev'n and Morn.
> (VII. 252)

> So Ev'n
> And Morning *Chorus* sung the second Day.
> (VII. 274–75)

> So Ev'n and Morn recorded the Third Day.
> (VII. 338)

With these two actions established, ensuing events can be located quite simply because of Milton's preciseness regarding them. The War in Heaven lasts three days and nights. It begins on the morning of the second day and comes to an end at dawn on the fourth day (VI. 748), when the Son routs Satan and his horde, casting them out of Heaven to fall "nine times the space that measures Day and Night" (I. 50), through Chaos to Hell's floor. Since Satan falls shortly after dawn,[11] and since Milton reverses his

10. Throughout this chapter I employ "day" metaphorically to indicate a unit of time, whether celestial or mundane, so "lik'ning spiritual to corporal forms."
11. Cirillo says that the Son drives the rebels from Heaven at noon, but there is no indication that Milton intended noon to be understood as the time of the rout of the Satanic crew. The Son ascends his chariot as "the third sacred Morn began to shine" (VI. 748). The reference to Mulciber's fall, which Cirillo cites, confirms the morning defeat.

usual verbal formula for describing the sequence of night and day in the line cited from Book I, it is logical to count the first day and night of his fall as the daylight hours of the fourth day and the evening hours of the fifth. Thus Satan's horde falls upon Hell's burning lake appropriately in the evening that begins the thirteenth day of the narrative. And if we recall Milton's reference to Mulciber's fall—"from Morn/To Noon he fell, from Noon to dewy Eve,/ . . . and with the setting Sun/Dropt from the Zenith like a falling Star" (I. 742–45)—we see that it tallies with these estimates, though in itself only a figurative statement based on ancient fable. In Hell they lie transfixed for an additional nine days. Presumably Satan raises his head to look balefully about him during the night that begins the twenty-second day. It is at this point that Milton chose to plunge into the midst of his narrative. The events immediately following Satan's rising are designated in time a bit vaguely, but not so much so that we are unable to work out a satisfactory relationship between them and the diurnal structure of events. Basically, the events suggest the passage of one night from the moment when Satan arises to the point when, flying upward toward the newly created universe, he sees "at last the sacred influence/Of light" that "from the walls of Heav'n/Shoots far into the bosom of dim Night/A glimmering dawn" (II. 1034–37). Time here as elsewhere in the universe outside the newly created world of man is only an approximation that allows us to perceive the relationship of events in our own perspective. If we accept this necessary and obvious distinction throughout, it seems reasonable to relate those events leading up to Satan's encounter with Sin and Death as occurring essentially during the nighttime hours of the twenty-second day. Thus it is the dawn of the twenty-second day that we behold with Satan, as he wings his way upward at the close of Book II.

Once within the sphere of the world, Satan comes under

the influence of the Sun, and the temporal aspects of the poem become literal instead of figurative. Satan stands, for example, in the Sun at noon (IV. 564) and converses with Uriel. He flies to Eden and spies Adam and Eve for the first time in the late afternoon, shortly before "the Sun/Declin'd was hasting now with prone career/To th' Ocean Isles" (IV. 352–54). At nine o'clock—the evening that begins the twenty-third day—he sits at Eve's ear and troubles her sleep with a dream of temptation (IV. 776–77). The angelic guards find him at Eve's side and return with him to Gabriel. After a threatened scuffle, Satan flees "murmuring, and with him . . . the shades of night" (IV. 1015). It is the morning of the twenty-third day.

We are not told how long Satan is away from Eden until Book IX, when Milton says that Satan returned to the garden on the eighth night after flying around the globe of earth for the "space of seven continu'd nights" (IX. 64, 67). The time designation is exact, but it has hitherto led to confusion about the time-scheme of *Paradise Lost,* confusion that has upset calculations to correlate the poetic chronology with the various patterns of time and event defined in the hexameral tradition. To my knowledge, previous commentators have read the phrase "seven continu'd nights" as if it meant seven twenty-four-hour periods. This is surely not what Milton intends. In the first place it is Milton's habit, as we have seen, to speak of elements of each twenty-four-hour period as days *and* nights: see, for example, the description of Satan's fall through chaos to Hell's floor (I. 50). Of more importance, however, is the fact that Satan returns to Eden after his flight of seven continuous nights during the darkness of the eighth night. Seven or eight continuous 24-hour periods would, of course, bring Satan back to Eden at dawn. As he fled at dawn, so he would return at dawn. If Milton means, however, that Satan stayed in the darkness for seven continuous nights, or three-and-a-half 24-hour periods, returning on the eighth night, he would correctly enter Eden the second time sometime during the night that begins the twenty-seventh day of the narrative, the day of the Fall.[12]

The pattern of events that occurs from dawn on the twenty-seventh day until nightfall is quite precisely related in time by Milton. Adam and Eve rise at dawn, discuss the need to divide their labor, go forth separately agreeing to meet at mid-day. But as noon approaches Eve is tempted by Satan and falls (IX. 739–40, 780–81). Adam falls shortly thereafter, and the two indulge their new-felt passions until gross sleep overwhelms them. Late in the afternoon (X. 92–95) the Son finds them in the garden and pronounces judgment on them for their transgression. There follows the long night of lamentation, in which Adam and Eve finally resign themselves to God's providence and fall to repentant prayer. It is, at once, a dark night of the soul and the beginning of a new day, a day in which Michael will show Adam a vision of the future history of man, allowing him the consolation of time in place of the timeless innocence that had been his. On the twenty-eighth and last day of its chronology, the poem closes with Adam and Eve's departure from the garden.

12. McColley, Qvarnström, and Fowler all mistakenly conceive of the Satanic flight from Eden as occupying seven 24-hour periods. McColley thus calculates that the overall time scheme of *Paradise Lost* comprises 31 days. Both Qvarnström and Fowler find the time scheme to be designed to add up to the numerologically significant period of 33 days. What numerology gains, however, typology loses by this reckoning. The calculations of the latter critics lose sight of significant temporal parallels between the Fall and the Crucifixion, discussed above. The 33–day chronology may be summarized as follows:

1. Exaltation of Christ
2–4. War in Heaven
4–13. Fall through Chaos
13–22. Stupor in Hell
14–20. Creation
(19. Creation of man [Saturday])
22. Rebels awake
23. Satan enters Eden first time
24. First temptation; Satan expelled at midnight; Raphael's visit
24–31. Satan's night flight
32. Satan's return; fall of Adam and Eve [Friday]
33. Expulsion from Eden at noon.

In strict chronology the action of the poem takes place, then, in the equivalent of twenty-eight days from the beginning of time, when the Father elevates the Son, until the moment when Adam and Eve descend from the garden, the world all before them. And yet Milton does not merely present the pattern of time chronologically. As I have indicated, Milton embraces the twenty-eight-day period principally through flashback, by which he can establish a number of particular temporal stresses that have little to do with chronology as such and a great deal to do with symbolic time. In this we can say that the poem's time begins when Satan raises his head from the burning lake (I. 53). From that moment until the end of the poem, the temporal stress is symbolic and relates closely to the hexameral tradition, which claimed that the Fall occurred on the eighth day after Creation, on a Friday, and at such time as to prefigure the Crucifixion.

Biblical commentators had long argued the question of how long Adam and Eve remained in the Garden. It was a crucial question in terms of the whole temporal structure of the Creation, quite naturally, and it was particularly perplexing since the accounts in Genesis gave no suggestion of time-when in relation to the Fall. According to Grant McColley, though a number of suggestions were made as to how long Adam was in the garden, ranging in time from 12 hours to 33 years, the accounts shared the concept that, however long Adam was there, his stay reinforced the notion that Christ was the second Adam, taking on himself all man's sins that descended to him through the original sin in Adam. In summarizing the various traditions, McColley points out that the version of the Fall that believed Adam remained in the garden only 12 hours became over the centuries "the most authoritative of all" (p. 160). The primary justification for this was the parallel established between the Fall and the twelve hours of Christ's crucifixion. Christ came before Pilate in the morning and was placed on the cross at the third hour. At the sixth hour—that is, at noon—darkness descended, the same hour that Eve ate the apple, and at the ninth hour the Son called to the Father, the time that God called Adam to judgment in the garden. In the evening Christ was taken from the cross just as Adam had been ejected from the garden in the evening of the day he fell. As Adam was created on Friday, the sixth day of the week, so Christ died on Friday.

There is no reason to doubt that Milton knew this tradition, and there is some internal evidence that he may have intended the comparison between the Crucifixion and Fall in the temporal sequence established in Books IX and X. Milton indicates that Adam and Eve were in the garden, however, for a period of time considerably longer than this tradition would allow. Returning to McColley, we learn that the "second most influential interpretation" of the length of time that Adam was in Paradise claimed that he fell "on the eighth day of his creation, that day seven-night wherein he was made."[13] McColley feels that Milton employed both traditions in *Paradise Lost*, suggesting the first by having Satan present Eve a dream of temptation on the evening of their first day in *Paradise*, and the second by the obvious time-lapse from Satan's discovery until his return, a lapse that McColley wrongly believes to be seven days. In Milton's time scheme, however, McColley's first suggestion seems inappropriate. If Satan were to be considered as tempting Eve on the night of the creation of man—that is, on the night of the sixth day—it forces us to identify Raphael's mission to the garden in which he explains the War in Heaven and the Creation, as occurring on the original Sabbath, a day of rest for all. Moreover, if Satan were at Eve's ear on the sixth day, it would mean that Adam and Eve actually fell in Milton's scheme of things in the middle of the week, rather than on Friday as tradition had it. If the

13. McColley, p. 160; the statement is from David Pareus *In Genesis Mosis Commentarius* (Frankfort, 1615).

Fall occurs on Friday, Raphael's visit must be on the preceding Monday, at the very least three days after the creation of man and, at the most, some 14 days after his creation.

The principal problem in relation to the precise date after the Creation on which Milton meant Adam to fall arises because of Milton's own impreciseness about the time when the Creation began. It must occur sometime between the beginning of the fifth day while Satan falls through space and the twenty-second day when Satan enters Eden and first sees Adam and Eve. We have no way of knowing when during these seventeen days Milton intended to place the Creation. It is clear, however, from Raphael's remark to Adam about his "voyage uncouth" to Hell's gate the day Adam was created (VIII. 228ff.) that the Creation takes place during the Rebels' stunned, painful days lying on the burning lake, perhaps near the moment of their awakening, when the first anguished stirrings of their new being animate them. And if we recall the words of Chaos to Satan concerning the various encroachments on his kingdom as a result of the War in Heaven, it seems that Milton thought of Creation as following after Satan's fall:

> I upon my Frontiers here
> Keep residence; if all I can will serve,
> That little which is left so to defend,
> Encroacht on still through our intestine broils
> Weak'ning the Sceptre of old *Night:* first Hell
> Your dungeon stretching far and wide beneath;
> Now lately Heaven and Earth, another World
> Hung o'er my Realm.
>   (II. 998–1005)

Thus the Creation takes place at some time between the beginning of the 14th day-night period and the beginning of the 22nd. If we work back from the presumed Friday of the Fall in Eden, the only day possible for Creation to have begun in Milton's scheme appears to be Sunday, the fifteenth day after the Elevation of the Son and the midpoint of the poem's temporal structure. Thus man would be created on Friday, the twentieth day of the poem's sequence; the twenty-first day would be the first Sabbath, followed immediately, on the evening of the twenty-second day, by Satan's renewed rising against God.

It would seem, then, that Milton accepts the second most influential tradition on the length of time Adam and Eve were in the garden. They fall eight days after their creation. The temporal scheme of the day of the Fall suggests several parallels with the Crucifixion, primarily in the insistence on the noon hour of Fall and the late-afternoon judgment. Milton shifts his emphasis away from the expulsion at evening, however, and allows Adam and Eve to go out from the Garden after they have been refreshed mentally and physically by means of the vision of the future. They leave Paradise in peace on the Sabbath, the seventh day, itself an image of the seventh age of man, termed "our Sabbath" by St. Augustine. The flow of sequential time has been involved in the manipulation of symbolic time, when specific acts break into the smooth flow and charge it with new meaning. In this sequence, time begins when Satan raises his head from Hell's floor and ends when Adam and Eve depart from the Garden. The time that elapses is just seven days. Moments of crisis have been made to fit with a sense of symbolic, creative time. In a poetic sense *chronos* and *kairos* become consonant. And yet the poem also expands vastly beyond time to embrace both the temporal structure of the cosmos and the atemporal aspects of eternity.

Thus *Paradise Lost* can define time historically and mystically. On the first level, we recognize that all of Milton's narrative was for him and his audience of the order of historical fact. The historical stretch of events emphasizes as well a conceptualization of the world and time. In his vision of the future, for example, Raphael provides Adam with a chronicle of Old Testament events leading up to the coming of Messiah. Beyond this, Raphael alludes to the final "dissolution" of the world at Judgment, when each man will receive his just reward. Thus Adam learns of the ages of man that will follow him. In accord with Christian notions of time and history, those ages will be seven, paralleling the days of Creation and reflecting the mystical seven that signified eternity and perfection. Milton marks off these ages quite clearly, the first being from the Creation itself to the Flood. This is the matter of the historical vision provided in Book XI. Book XII describes in quick succession the age from the flood to Abraham (XII. 111), from Abraham to David (XII. 315), from David to the Babylonian Captivity (XII. 348), from the Captivity till the birth of Christ (XII. 360), and from the Nativity to the Millennium (XII. 458), when the Son

> thence shall come
> When this world's dissolution shall be ripe,
> With glory and power to judge both quick and dead,
> To judge th' unfaithful dead, but to reward
> His faithful, and receive them into bliss,
> Whether in Heav'n or Earth, for then the Earth
> Shall all be Paradise, far happier place
> Than this of *Eden*, and far happier days.

This seventh day, "our Sabbath," shall be brought to a close, as St. Augustine says,

> not by an evening, but by the Lord's day, as an eighth and eternal day, consecrated by the resurrection of Christ and prefiguring the eternal repose not only of the spirit, but also of the body. There we shall rest and see, see and love, love and praise. This is what shall be in the end without end.[14]

These are the "ages of endless date" that Michael describes, which will follow judgment

14. *The City of God,* trans. Marcus Dods (New York, 1950), p. 867.

> at return
> Of him so lately promis'd to thy aid,
> The Woman's seed, obscurely then foretold,
> Now ampler known thy Savior and thy Lord,
> Last in the Clouds from Heav'n to be reveal'd
> In glory of the Father, to dissolve
> *Satan* with his perverted World, then raise
> From the conflagrant mass, purg'd and refin'd,
> New Heav'ns, new Earth, Ages of endless date
> Founded in righteousness and peace and love,
> To bring forth fruits Joy and eternal Bliss.
>   (XII. 541–51)

They comprise the Lord's day, the "eighth and eternal day." And though *Paradise Lost* ends with the departure from Eden on the seventh day, Milton has provided a haunting allusion to the final vision of time at the moment of departure. As Adam and Eve prepare to leave, the Cherubim descend

> On the ground
> Gliding meteorous, as Ev'ning Mist
> Ris'n from a River o'er the marish glides,
> And gathers ground fast at the Laborer's heel
> Homeward returning.
>   (XII. 628–32)

It is not evening. It is only an image of evening in the midst of this, the seventh day of Milton's poem. This day, which brings with it the descent from the garden and the beginning of the long homeward trek, "shall be brought to a close not by an evening, but by the Lord's day . . . of eternal repose."[15]

---

15. The seven/eight day pattern of *Paradise Lost* provides another striking parallel with the *Commedia*. Writing of Dante's time scheme, Vincent Hopper says:

> The 6 days consumed in traversing Hell and Purgatory suggest strongly the journey of humanity through the 6 earthly ages. The seventh is the Final Sabbath of the world, the age of the Final Resurrection, and accordingly the seventh day finds Dante in the Earthly Paradise. At noon of this day he rises

More than mere dry historical data resulting in an anti-climactic close to the epic, as some critics have felt, the final books reaffirm the symmetry of the whole poem in a temporal as well as a spatial manner. I have already pointed out the spatial structure of balance and reversal that exists between Book I and XII in relation to the historical data. The fallen angels catalogued in Book I find their counterparts in the biblical heroes described in the account of the ages of man. But there is, of course, a crucial difference that the historical perspective of the last books makes clear. The fallen angels appear to man in many guises and under many fictions. They are in a sense fabulous, whereas the events and personages of the last books of the epic are historical. The distinction is one of long standing; Isidore of Seville makes it clearly in his *Etymologiae*. Following such writers as Jerome and Cassiodorus, Isidore describes under the heading of *fabula* those things which are pure invention, whereas *historia* provides a narrative "rei gestae," of things that really happened. Though *historia* may be of three kinds, the daily report or *ephemeris*, the monthly summary

---

to the Eternal Paradise, having ascending from the temporal to the spiritual world. In the same seventh day, he moves upward through all the heavens. Before the poet's visions in the eighth heaven of the redeemed, there is a transition to the "eighth age . . . the age of Final Redemption, eternal and timeless." (*Medieval Number Symbolism*, p. 199.)

Michael Fixler, in "The Apocalypse in *Paradise Lost*," provides a provocative, if tentative analysis of the structural and conceptual relationship of *Paradise Lost* to Revelation, which is "cryptic," depending for comprehension on "special knowledge as the privilege of the regenerate understanding, which alone was adequately suited to penetrate prophetic mysteries" (pp. 136–37). Although Fixler describes a structural principle for Milton's epic very different from that which I have been examining, he stresses the sevenfold division of *Paradise Lost* that, he feels, corresponds to the seven visions of the Apocalypse. And he remarks, significantly from my point of view, that to "understand the relation between *Paradise Lost* and Revelation one must bear in mind that Milton's materials were essentially hexameral, dealing with the week of Creation, whereas the Apocalypse was eschatological, with a sequence of visions concerned with the 'week' that takes historical Creation into the timelessness of the millennium" (p. 147). To my mind, the question confronting the reader at this point is whether he is dealing with, in Fixler's proposition, a rival structural principle or rather with another indication of the marvelous consonances in Milton's epic.

or *kalendaria*, and *annalis*, which sweep over the years, the real distinction to be made is between fiction, or fable, and history, or fact.[16] This is the distinction that lies at the heart of the contrast between the seven ages of man and those fabulous, or feigned appearances of the Satanic demons throughout history. Their incursions are real enough in point of fact, but their significance in the divine scheme of things is as fable. They relate only indirectly to the true history of man. The design is God's; the demons are merely the most artificial kind of factors, whose activities ultimately are insubstantial shadows cast by the half-light of fable. The harsh irony is most apparent when we recall the need of the demons to assume numerous shapes and guises in order to approach man. They enforce their fabulous nature in the very manner of their presence in the universe. The more they appear, the less real they are; each act diminishes them. In the universal history with which he concludes his epic, therefore, Milton reintroduces the demons from time to time, but they are as "chaff which the wind driveth away." They are insubstantial when set against the concrete working out of man's destiny in a historical perspective.

And yet, having said this, we must quickly remind ourselves of the mythic sense of return that pervades the last books of *Paradise Lost*. Through a kind of economy by conflation, Milton achieves at once the sense of the stretch of time, periodicized, and the turn of time upon itself with something of the force of cyclical renewal. As we watch Adam and Eve leave the garden and descend into Eden with the world before them, we are aware of the loss, it is true, but we are just as aware—probably more so—of the beginning that confronts all men. The spatial and temporal

16. Curtius, *European Literature and the Latin Middle Ages*, trans. Willard Trask, Bollingen series 36, (New York, 1953), pp. 450–53. The distinction between kinds of history bears an interesting relationship to the temporal patterns of *Paradise Lost*, recounting the daily occurrences of Eden, the calendar occurrences of the twenty-eight days, and the annals of future time.

perspective has been set before us with a concreteness that we cannot deny, but also with a softening sense of promise. Through the data of existence and by an acceptance of change, man can ameliorate his sense of loss with the reality of return.

This is the temporal insistence that Milton has pursued throughout his poem by means of imagery that conflates time and provides something of a historical overview. I have spoken of this earlier in another context (see chapter 1), and little remains to be done here beyond reminding ourselves that the great epic similes expand by a series of allusions that define the temporal relevance of each element in God's scheme. The marvelous Vallombrosa image in Book I provides a case in point. The image describes Satan as he moves toward the shore in Hell, a specific moment and movement within the dramatic structure of the poem. But the image ranges in time forward to contemporary events as it compares Satan's spear to the mast of a seventeenth-century capital ship; and, as the size of his shield is likened to the moon, it reminds Milton through a series of associations of his youthful visit to the valley of the Arno and the beauty of the autumn, now irrevocably lost to him. The image also likens the fallen hordes to the broken chivalry of the Pharaoh destroyed in the Red Sea during his pursuit of the Jews. All these temporal allusions are brought together in the one epic simile. Beyond them, the broader references to autumn, Orion, and the tides of the Red Sea provide the image with a generality of detail that touches any age and suggests thereby the relevance of the specific moment in Hell to all men.

All this is clear enough. But in considering the overall temporal effects that Milton seems bent on achieving, we realize, as I said earlier, that the complexity of these images provides him with a means of suggesting, by human analogy, something of the quality of God's time, which involves historical range in an atemporal medium. It is in this sense that the central action of the poem, the Elevation of the Son, must be understood, as William B. Hunter, Jr., has shown recently.[17]

Addressing himself to the problem raised in the Elevation of the Son and the particular confusion of the time sequence that results—not to mention the doctrinal difficulties related to the subordinationist principle explicit in the Exaltation—Hunter finds a solution to the problem that suggests a new understanding of certain events of the epic. He shows, in particular, how, in the initiating actions of *Paradise Lost*, the exaltation of the Son and the resulting war in Heaven, Milton is presenting simultaneously

> three events from three very different points in time: first, the surface narrative of the fall of the angels, which took place before the foundation of the world; second, the defeat of Satan and his fellow devils described in the book of Revelation, which will take place at the end of time; and third and most important, the exaltation of the Son of God, which took place concomitantly with his resurrection as the incarnate God-man. All three of these events, from the beginning, middle and end of time, are to be viewed as being simultaneously and metaphorically present in the one narrative framework. Unifying this disparate material is a single theme: the victorious exaltation of the Son of God. (pp. 223–24)

Hunter's whole discussion is of immense importance to an understanding of *Paradise Lost*. No summary will really suffice to do it justice. For our purposes here, however, it may be enough to say that Milton creates a sense of the eternal vision of God in representing the three events in one image. As God is eternal, so all time is immediately present to Him. Things accomplished by God have been

17. "Milton on the Exaltation of the Son," *ELH* 36 (1969) :215–31. For others who have previously investigated similar aspects of the vision of exaltation, see Mother Mary Christopher Pecheux, "The Conclusion of Book VI of *Paradise Lost*, *SEL* 3 (1963): 109–17, and John Shawcross, "The Son in His Ascendance: A Reading of *Paradise Lost*, *MLQ* 27 (1966): 388–401.

with Him from eternity. It is only in relation to our mortal scheme of time data that chronological distinctions are necessary or relevant. Thus, in the Exaltation: "the Son *virtually* offered himself as sacrifice . . . a sacrifice which actually is accomplished in the 'fulness of time' " (p. 224). The central moment of the poem then becomes the central doctrine and justification of Milton's art. This section of the poem is, as Hunter shows,

> one enormous metaphor . . . which has three different temporal interpretations, three different events which will later be realized in time and which collectively span all of time. . . . All three events show him victorious over the forces of evil. (p. 225)

The image of the War in Heaven corresponds to the three days the Son was under the power of death at his Crucifixion, and mirrors the final war described in Revelation 12. Linked with this and supporting Hunter's thesis is the specific diurnal relationship established by Milton between the Fall and Crucifixion, and between the Elevation and Creation, which events, it will be seen from a study of the time-chart (Fig. 6), occur with a consonance suggestive of the ultimate symbolic consonance by which all events are one in meaning and time in God's scheme. It is a symbolic scheme—defined by Cirillo in terms of the noon-midnight patterns through which we perceive noon to be "the perfect time of day, the image of eternity" (p. 375)—that defines all in the one, eternal moment of victory over evil.

In the central image, therefore, Milton provides us with the final, transcendent sense of Good conquering Evil, of the Eternal subsuming the temporal in "heav'n's great Year." The final justification is exactly that, a justifying or an exact adjusting, of the temporal scheme of the poem with the spatial structure adumbrated in the image of the circle. Both are worked out, in a reasonable human equivalency, to perfection. As in life so in the poem, the "terror

of history," the exhaustive sense of "one thing after another," gives way before the sense of return. Time and
space, which are interrelated in history, are given shape by
the poet's creative hand, and that shape offers a vague
sense of the ultimate collocation of time and space in the
Eternal. The whole of mundane existence is under the eye
of God and can be called a shape. There is a plan, that is,
however dimly we perceive it, that comprehends both time
and space as they finally resolve themselves in the ultimate
center that is God. Richard Crashaw captures the sense of
how time and space are involved with each other in the
ultimate and original essence of God:

> To Thee, thou Day of night! thou east of west!
> Lo we at last have found the way.
> To thee, the world's great universal east.
> The Generall and indifferent Day,
> All-circling point. All cent'ring sphear.
> . . . .
> O little all! in thy embrace
> The world lyes warm, and likes his place.
> Nor does his full Globe fail to be
> Kist on Both his cheeks by Thee.[18]

Thus in time as well as in space the poem moves forward
and circularly, graphically achieving a suggestion of beginning again, allowing us to start out as do Adam and Eve,
better for the "new aquist" that has come with the experience of the poem.

---

18 *In the glorious Epiphany of Our Lord God. A hymn sung as by the Three Kings. Poems,*
ed. L. C. Martin (Oxford, 1957), pp. 254–55.

1D	Sunday:	Elevation of the Son	
2N	Monday:	Satan withdraws to the north	
D		Outbreak of war	
3N	Tuesday:	Satan invents cannon	
D		War continues	
4N	Wednesday:	God puts the battle in the hands of His Son	
D		Son routs Satan at dawn; Satan begins to fall	
5N–12D		Rebels fall "Nine times the space that measures Day and Night" (I. 50)	
13N	Friday:	Satan and horde land in Hell; lie transfixed in Hell nine days	
D			
14N	Saturday:		
D			
15N	Sunday:		
D		Creation begins (1st day)	
20N	Friday:		
D		Adam and Eve created (6th day)	
21N	Saturday:		
D		The first Sabbath	

(The point at which Milton begins *Paradise Lost:* main units of time in poem.)

22N	Sunday:	Satan rouses himself; flies upward toward the "glimmering dawn" (close of Book II)	1st day
D			
23N	Monday:	Satan found at Eve's ear	
D		Satan flees murmuring at dawn (end of Book IV)	2nd day
			3d, 4th, 5th days
27N	Friday:	Satan returns to Eden	
D		Eve tempted at noon; Adam falls shortly after; judgment	6th day
28N	Saturday:	Night of lamentation	
D		Vision of future; Adam and Eve depart from Eden refreshed (image of evening)	7th day

Time Scheme of *Paradise Lost*

FIGURE 6

Conclusion

Though the question remains as to what extent Milton expected his readers to perceive these signs of "symbolic symmetry" with which he endowed his creation, it is in keeping with the general character of the work, it seems to me, that its structure in large part fulfills the meaning. How could it reasonably be otherwise? The poem attempts microscopically to reflect the perfect symmetry of the macrocosm created in time and space. In a sense the spatial pattern and temporal scheme are akin in their function to Renaissance notions about the mysterious wisdom of the universe reflected in all great works of the hand and mind. Milton has constructed his poem in such a way that anagogically it stands as a marvelous hieroglyph of the divine plan and its justice. Events move forward in time and *seemingly* repeat themselves, yet each is different and all are circumscribed within the unending time that is at once the symbol and essence of the creator. The temporal plan relates to the spatial design and compares with it in artistic and coneptural perfection. The action of the poem takes place in seven units of time, like the Creation itself, the seventh embracing Adam and Eve's departure in peace from the Garden. The poem closes as it began, in the midst of things. God's time is circular, unending, formal, perfect, containing the multitudinous lines of men's lives. The poet's time partakes of both. Temporally and spatially, Milton

endeavors to make his own poetic universe as nearly perfect as he can in accordance with his perception of the
divine interrelatedness of time and eternity, of space and
spaciousness, of the finite and infinite.

Whether we look at the spatial or the temporal aspects
of the poem, the sheer weight of detail suggests how
strongly Milton conceptualized, formalized, indeed, visual-
ized his epic. It provides, that is, a clear insight into the
poet's methods of composition as well as his notions of life.
Obviously, creation is for Milton a product of time and
painstaking labor through which he finally fashions a poem
that is both emblem and imitation of the divine creator.
Poetic fury has little, if any place in mystical composition.
Though, as Whaler reminds us, we have virtually no direct
evidence defining the methods and secrets of Milton's art
(p. 82), the circumstantial evidence that may be adduced
from the preceding investigation of the structure of *Paradise
Lost* suits well with the data we have. Speaking of the elaborate metrical patterns he believes are in evidence throughout *Paradise Lost*, Whaler summarizes one important aspect
of our understanding of Milton's poetic method:

> It follows also that if symbolic responses are present, based on
> progressions covering a goodly number of metric lines, then
> Milton must have composed his verse—as his biographer says
> he did—by dictating a more or less sustained group at every
> sitting, indeed an entire rounded paragraph whenever possi-
> ble. He did not create as Virgil did, line by line, nor as Shakes-
> peare did, "with that easinesse, that wee have scarce received
> from him a blot in his papers." Nor are we to understand in any
> literal sense Milton's tribute to his Muse, who he says "in-
> spires/Easy my unpremeditated verse." Easy—yes, in the mor-
> ning's outpour of ten to forty lines. But he takes the rest of the
> day to enrich them with after thoughts, to file and emend, to
> "pencil it over with all the curious touches of art, even to the
> perfection of a faultless picture." (p. 83)

To this very fine account of the way one perceives Milton
composing his epic, I would add only this point. The fact

of Milton's blindness will inevitably influence the way he perceives and sets about his work. It goes without saying, I believe, that a blind man's whole "visual" field is internal. Over a period of time for the poet such internal vision would naturally be brought to bear on the relationship of objects and ideas. It would produce an ability to "see" how disparate or unrelated elements would ultimately fit together in much the way, as I understand it, an expert in building a dry wall can visualize relationships in hunting out stone. Now, for about fifteen years Milton was forced by his blindness to visualize internally that poem which had been with him from youth. Like Meursault in his prison cell, Milton must daily have exercised his memory in imagining the elements of his poetic world. That the structural device of the circle suited his design thematically is fairly obvious, I think. That it could also aid him mnemonically may have been fortuitous but no less important for that. One could go on at length romanticizing the image of the blind bard tirelessly creating his masterpiece, imbuing his poem with a thousand signs whose intricate beauty like some mysterious web might never be seen, even by members of that small "fit audience." But the ultimate audience is God Himself, to whom Milton renders this "true account." In the end it is enough to say, then, that mystical methods of composition suit well with the needs of the epic and its poet. How rich a comment on both is the great hymn to heavenly light, which concludes with its own consolation:

> thou Celestial Light
> Shine inward, and the mind through all her powers
> Irradiate, there plant eyes, all mist from thence
> Purge and disperse, that I may see and tell
> Of things invisible to mortal sight.
> (III. 51–55)

Selected Bibliography

Adams, Robert. *Ikon: John Milton and the Modern Critics.* Ithaca, N.Y., 1955.

Allen, Don Cameron. *Mysteriously Meant; the Rediscovery of Pagan Symbolism and Allegorical Interpretation in the Renaissance.* Baltimore, Md., 1970.

Augustinus, Saint Aurelius, Bishop of Hippo. *The City of God.* Translated by Marcus Dods. New York, 1950.

Austin, Herbert. "From Matter to Spirit." *MLN* 38 (1923): 140–48.

———. "The Arrangement of Dante's 'Purgatorial Reliefs.'" *PMLA* 47 (1932): 1–9.

Barker, Arthur. "Structural Pattern in *Paradise Lost.*" *Philological Quarterly* 28 (1949): 17–30.

Barr, James. *Biblical Words for Time.* London, 1962.

Bassett, S. E. *The Poetry of Homer.* Sather Classical Lectures, vol. 15. Berkeley, Calif., 1958.

Blanchard, Sheila. "Structural Patterns in *Paradise Lost.*" Dissertation, University of Rochester, 1966.

Bush, Douglas. "Calculus Racked Him." *SEL* 6 (1966): 1–6.

Cassirer, Ernst. *The Philosophy of Symbolic Forms.* Translated by Ralph Manheim. 3 vols. New Haven, Conn. 1955.

Cirillo, Albert. "Noon-Midnight and the Temporal Structure of *Paradise Lost.*" *ELH* 29 (1962): pp. 372–95.

Colie, Rosalie. "Time and Eternity: Paradox and Structure in *Paradise Lost.*" *Journal of the Warburg and Courtauld Institute* 23 (1960): 127–38.

Cope, Jackson. *The Metaphoric Structure of* Paradise Lost. Baltimore, Md., 1962.

Cummings, R. M. "Two Sixteenth-Century Notices of Numerical Composition in Virgil's *Aeneid.*" *N&Q* 16, n.s. (1969): 26–27.

Donahue, Charles. "Summation," in *Critical Approaches to Medieval Literature; Selected Papers from the English Institute, 1958–59.* Edited by Dorothy Bethurum. New York, 1960.

Donne, John. *The Sermons of John Donne.* Edited by E. M. Simpson and George R. Porter. Berkeley, Calif., 1953.

Eliade, Mircea. *The Myth of the Eternal Return.* Translated by Willard Trask. Bolligen series 46. New York, 1954.

Ferry, Anne Davidson. *Milton's Epic Voice: The Narrator in* Paradise Lost. Cambridge, Mass., 1963.

Fish, Stanley Eugene. *Surprised by Sin: The Reader in* Paradise Lost. New York, 1967.

Fixler, Michael. *Milton and the Kingdoms of God.* London, 1964.

———. "The Apocalypse within *Paradise Lost,*" in *New Essays on* Paradise Lost. Edited by Thomas Kranidas. Berkeley, Calif., 1969, pp. 131–78.

Fludd, Robert. *Mosaicall Philosophy, grounded upon the essential truth or eternal sapience.* London, 1659.

Fowler, Alastair. *Triumphal Forms: Structural Patterns in Elizabethan Poetry.* Cambridge, 1970.

Frye, Northrop. *Anatomy of Criticism.* Princeton, 1957.

———. *Five Essays on Milton's Epics.* London, 1966.

Galilei, Galileo. *Le Opere di Galileo Galilei.* Edited by E. Albèri. 16 vols. Florence, 1842–56.

Gardner, Dame Helen. *A Reading of* Paradise Lost. Oxford, 1965.

Geymonat, Ludovico. *Galileo Galilei. A Biography and Inquiry into his Philosophy of Science.* Translated by Stillman Drake. New York, 1965.

Gilbert, Allan H. "Milton and Galileo." *SP* 19 (1922): 152–85.

Harris, Fletcher. *The Intellectual Development of John Milton.* 2 vols. Urbana, Ill., 1956.

Havens, Raymond Dexter. *The Influence of Milton on English Poetry.* Cambridge, Mass., 1922.

Hieatt, A. Kent. *Time's Endless Monument: The Symbolism of the Numbers in Spenser's Epithalamion.* New York, 1960.

Hopper, Vincent Foster. *Medieval Number Symbolism*. New York. 1938.

Hunter, William B. Jr. "Milton on the Exaltation of the Son." *ELH* 36 (1969): 215–31.

Kermode, Frank. *The Sense of an Ending: Studies in the Theory of Fiction*. Oxford, 1967.

Koyré, Alexandre. *From the Closed World to the Infinite Universe*. Baltimore, Md., 1957.

Langer, Susanne, K. *Mind: An Essay on Human Feeling*. Baltimore, Md., 1967.

Leisegang, Hans. *Denkformen*. Berlin, 1928.

Lewis, C. S. *A Preface to* Paradise Lost. Oxford, 1942.

Lieb, Michael. *The Dialectics of Creation: Patterns of Birth and Regeneration in* Paradise Lost. Amherst, Mass., 1970.

Lubac, Father Henri de. *Exégèse médiévale, les quatre sens de l'Écriture*. 4 vols. Paris, 1959–64.

MacCaffrey, Isabel Gamble. Paradise Lost *as "Myth"*. Cambridge, Mass., 1959.

McColley, Grant. Paradise Lost *and the Hexameral Tradition*. Chicago, 1940.

Madsen, William G. *From Shadowy Types to Truth: Studies in Milton's Symbolism*. New Haven, Conn. 1968.

_____. "The Idea of Nature in Milton's Poetry." *Three Studies in the Renaissance*. . . . New Haven, 1958.

Mahood, M. M. *Poetry and Humanism*. Port Washington, N.Y., 1950.

Manley, Frank. "Milton and the Beasts of the Field." *MLN* 76 (1961): 398–403.

Martz, Louis, L. *The Paradise Within. Studies in Vaughan, Traherne, and Milton*. New Haven, Conn., 1964.

Milton, John. *Complete Poems and Major Prose*. Edited by Merritt Y. Hughes. New York, 1957.

_____. *The Works of John Milton*. Edited by Frank A. Patterson, et al. 20 vols. New York, 1931–40.

Nicolson, Marjorie. "Milton and the Telescope." *ELH* 2 (1935): 1–32.

Otis, Brooks. *Virgil: A Study in Civilized Poetry*. Oxford, 1964.

Patrides, C. A. "The Numerological Approach to Cosmic Order during the English Renaissance." *Isis* 49 (1958): 391–97.

Pecheux, Mother Mary Christopher. "The Conclusion of Book VI of *Paradise Lost.*" *SEL* 3 (1963): 109–17.

Peter, John. *A Critique of* Paradise Lost. New York, 1960.

Plato. *The Republic of Plato.* Translated by Allan Bloom. New York, 1968.

Poulet, Georges. *Les Métamorphoses du cercle.* Paris, 1961.

Price, Martin. *To the Palace of Wisdom: Studies in Order and Energy from Dryden to Blake.* New York, 1964.

Prince, F. T. *The Italian Element in Milton's Verse.* Oxford, 1954.

Puttenham, George. *The Arte of English Poesie.* Edited by Gladys D. Willcock and Alice Walker. Cambridge, 1936.

Qvarnström, Gunnar. *The Enchanted Palace: Some Structural Aspects of* Paradise Lost. Stockholm, 1967.

Rajan, Balachandra. Paradise Lost *and the Seventeenth Century Reader.* London, 1947.

Ricks, Christopher. *Milton's Grand Style.* Oxford, 1963.

Røstvig, Maren-Sofie. *The Hidden Sense: Milton and the Neoplatonic Method of Numerical Composition.* Oslo, 1963.

Ryken, Leland. *The Apocalyptic Vision in* Paradise Lost. Ithaca, N.Y., 1970.

Samuel, Irene. *Dante and Milton: The* Commedia *and* Paradise Lost. Ithaca, N.Y., 1966.

Seznec, Jean. *The Survival of the Pagan Gods.* New York, 1953.

Shawcross, John T. "The Balanced Structure of *Paradise Lost.*" *SP* 62 (1965): 696–718.

———. "The Son in His Ascendance: A Reading of *Paradise Lost,*" *MLQ* 27 (1966): 388–401.

———. "Some Literary Uses of Numerology." *Hartford Studies in Literature* 1, no. 1 (1969): 50–62.

———. "*Paradise Lost* and the Theme of Exodus." *Milton Studies* 2 (1970): 3–26.

Sidney, Sir Philip. *The Defence of Poesie.* Edited by Albert Feuillerat. Cambridge, 1923.

Singleton, Charles S. Commedia: *Elements of Structure.* In *Dante Studies* 1. Cambridge, Mass., 1965.

Spitzer, Leo. Review of *Le Haut Livre du Graal: Perlesvaus,* edited by W. A. Nitze and others. *MLN* 53 (1938): pp. 604–8.

_____. "Le Style 'Circulaire'." *MLN* 55 (1940): 495–99.

Stapleton, Lawrence. "Milton's Conception of Time." *Harvard Theological Review* 57 (1964): 9–21.

Strauss, Leo. *Persecution and the Art of Writing.* Glencoe, Ill. 1952.

Summers, Joseph. *George Herbert: His Religion and Art.* London, 1954.

Watkins, Walter B. C. *An Anatomy of Milton's Verse.* Baton Rouge, La., 1955.

Watson, J. R. "Divine Providence and the Structure of *Paradise Lost.*" *Essays in Criticism* 14 (1964): 148–55.

Whaler, James. *Counterpoint and Symbol. Anglistica* (Copenhagen) 6 (1956).

Whitman, Cedric. *Homer and the Heroic Tradition.* Cambridge, Mass., 1958.

Wittkower, Rudolf. *Architectural Principles of the Age of Humanism.* 2d ed. London, 1952.

Wittreich, Joseph, A., Jr. "Milton's 'Destin'd Urn': The Art of Lycidas." *PMLA* 84 (1969): 60–70.

INDEX

191